Be An Example: Godly Youth In the Bible

Evangeline Bibb

Cover Art by Daniel Tarr, IV

Book Illustrations by Chuck Fletcher

**All Scripture quotations are from the Authorized Version of the King James Bible.*

**All hymns cited are in the public domain*

ISBN # 9798676232320

"Let no man despise thy youth; but
be thou an example of the believers,
in word, in conversation, in charity,
in spirit, in faith, in purity."

1Timothy 4:12

Dedication

This book is lovingly dedicated to my parents, Charles and Linda Davis, who taught me the Word of God and led me to salvation in Jesus Christ. Their prayers, example, and teaching were used by the Spirit of God to plant within me a passion to study the Scriptures and a desire to share the truth of the Bible with others. It is this passion that has prompted me to write this book. Through all the failures and wanderings of my life, God has continually brought me back to His blessed Word and to these precious truths taught to me from childhood. I am eternally grateful to my parents for giving me a faithful and godly heritage to pass on to my own children. This book is further dedicated to my loving husband, Brooks, who has supported and encouraged me through every endeavor and has provided me with the freedom to pour my heart into our family and into the study of God's Word. I'm so grateful to him for his help, love, and constant provision. I cannot thank him enough for all that he does for me and for our family day after day.

I am eternally grateful for the truth of God's Word. The greatest dedication to be written must be to Him to whom all glory is due- the LORD God of Heaven. To Him we owe our life, our breath, and all things. I can testify with confidence, along with the saints of God whose lives are highlighted in these pages, that God is faithful. His promises never fail. His Word is true. He watches over His children. He rebukes and corrects them in love. He calls them back to His side and blesses their obedience with more grace and truth. He never fails. My prayer is that this study will serve to strengthen that same confidence in every reader's heart.

Table of Contents

<u>Preface</u>

Young people are faced with a daunting array of decisions during their growing-up years. These choices will affect the rest of their lives, creating habits, reputations, and belief systems that will determine the course of a young man's or young woman's personal history. The world offers many inspirations, both good and bad, for the choices young people must make. How can pre-teen, teenaged, or college-aged youth make solid, wise decisions that they will not regret in later years? How can they discern which examples to follow or which heroes to admire? How can they overcome the myriad of obstacles the world places in their way?

A young man asked similar questions many thousands of years ago, for youth in the past faced the same dilemmas the younger generations face today. Through God's grace and godly wisdom passed down from generations before him, this young man found a complete and dependable answer to his query:

Ps 119:9 "Wherewithal shall a young man cleanse his way? by taking heed *thereto* according to thy word."

The stories of young people who faced the difficult decisions of life by taking heed to God's Word are contained within these pages. By looking in God's Word at the examples of those in the past, today's youth can become examples for those who will come behind them in the future.

-Corrienna E. Tarr

Chapter 1: "The Life of Abel" (Part 1)

Memory Verse:

Hebrews 11:6 "But without faith *it is* impossible to please *him*: for he that cometh to God must believe that he is, and *that* he is a rewarder of them that diligently seek him."

Scripture Reading: Genesis 1-2

Key Lessons: Foundational truths concerning God, creation, man, and salvation

Have you ever wished you could be the very first person to do some great thing that the world would remember you for? That you could go down in history as a person who won a great battle, created an amazing invention, painted a masterpiece, or performed some great deed- something that would be written down and read by generations to come? Abel, a young man whose story is found in the Bible, was just such a person. His example is one we can all follow. In fact,

Be An Example

Abel was the very first example of a young person who chose to love God and follow His way, no matter the cost.

The story of Abel's life is found in Genesis 4, but to understand what he went through, we need to consider some things about his unique situation and family. In fact, the background of Abel's story began at the very dawn of creation, for he was the son of the very first man and woman- Adam and Eve. In Genesis 1, we find some very important truths concerning God Himself and the circumstances that formed the backdrop of Abel's life. In reality, these foundational truths form the background of all of our lives.

The Creation of the World: Genesis 1:1-2:

Ge 1:1-3 "In the beginning God created the heaven and the earth. And the earth was without form, and void; and darkness *was* upon the face of the deep. And the Spirit of God moved upon the face of the waters. And God said, Let there be light: and there was light."

Genesis 1:1-3 clearly states that God created the heaven and the earth by His powerful word; it also explains that the first step of God's creative work was to lay the foundations of the earth and heavens in preparation for all that would follow. This is what is meant by the statement "And the earth was without form and void; and darkness was upon the face of the deep." Like an artist stretches forth a canvas to begin a great masterpiece, God stretched forth the vastness of the heavens into which He would place the sun, the moon, the stars, and all the host of heaven. Like a potter takes a lump of clay, God brought forth the matter and water from which He would form the foundation of His beautiful world. The Spirit of God moved upon the face of the waters of the earth in readiness for the life-giving work to begin. The earth was "without form and void"- a shapeless lump of matter and water void of life. But then God said, "Let there be light." Glorious light shone forth upon that lifeless mass called earth. By God's word light shined out of the darkness!

God's wondrous work had just begun. By His word God brought forth all of the wondrous fruits of the earth, the amazing structures of the solar system and outer space, the living creatures of the sea, earth, and sky- and man himself:

Ps 33:6 "By the word of the LORD were the heavens made; and all the host of them by the breath of his mouth."

Isa 51:12-13 "I, *even* I, *am* he that comforteth you: who *art* thou, that thou shouldest be afraid of a man *that* shall die, and of the son of man *which* shall be made *as* grass; And forgettest the LORD thy maker, that hath stretched forth the heavens, and laid the foundations of the earth;"

Job 38:4-7 "Where wast thou when I laid the foundations of the earth? declare, if thou hast understanding. Who hath laid the measures thereof, if thou knowest? or who hath stretched the line upon it? Whereupon are the foundations thereof fastened? or who laid the corner stone thereof; When the morning stars sang together, and all the sons of God shouted for joy?"

Ps 104:4-5 "*Who* laid the foundations of the earth, *that* it should not be removed for ever. Thou coveredst it with the deep as *with* a garment: the waters stood above the mountains."

God stretched forth the heavens and created them by the breath of His mouth, and He laid the foundations of the earth by His powerful word.

A Spiritual Truth Illustrated in Creation:

In God's work of creation we see a wondrous picture of the work God does in the human heart through salvation. God sees a lifeless sinner- separated from Him and in spiritual darkness -and He shines the light of His glorious truth upon him; then God breathes His life-giving Spirit into that person, and makes him a living, new creature, full of life and beauty for God's glory. This is God's work of salvation through Jesus Christ for any person who is willing to trust in Him and respond to the light of God's truth. What was once a dead piece of clay becomes a new creation in Christ Jesus full of life and fruitfulness!

2Co 5:17 "Therefore if any man *be* in Christ, *he is* a new creature: old things are passed away; behold, all things are become new."

If you have not trusted Jesus Christ as Savior, He calls to you now. He shines the light of His truth upon you. If you will but turn to Him and call upon Him, He will give you eternal life. The Holy Spirit of God will breathe life into your soul and make you a new creature with a living relationship with God. God, by His power took the lifeless lump of clay and water, and transformed it into a beautiful creation full of life, and light, and fruitfulness. He filled the dark and empty canvas of the heavens with the glory of the sun, moon, and stars. In the same way, God can make a beautiful creation of your life if you will come to Him:

2Co 4:6 "For God, who commanded the light to shine out of darkness, hath shined in our hearts, to *give* the light of the knowledge of the glory of God in the face of Jesus Christ."

Joh 3:16 "For God so loved the world, that he gave his only begotten Son, that whosoever believeth in him should not perish, but have everlasting life."

Creation is a wondrous picture of salvation.

The Purpose for God's Creation:

Not only does the Bible tell us that God created the heavens and the earth by the word of His power; it also tells us why God created all of these things. God created all things for His own pleasure and glory to demonstrate His wisdom and power:

Col 1:16-17 "For by him were all things created, that are in heaven, and that are in earth, visible and invisible, whether *they be* thrones, or dominions, or principalities, or powers: all things were created by him, and for him: And he is before all things, and by him all things consist."

Re 4:11 "Thou art worthy, O Lord, to receive glory and honour and power: for thou hast created all things, and for thy pleasure they are and were created."

Ps 19:1 "The heavens declare the glory of God; and the firmament sheweth his handywork."

Ps 104:24 "O LORD, how manifold are thy works! in wisdom hast thou made them all: the earth is full of thy riches."

Ps 148:1-5 "Praise ye the LORD. Praise ye the LORD from the heavens: praise him in the heights. Praise ye him, all his angels: praise ye him, all his hosts. Praise ye him, sun and moon: praise him, all ye stars of light. Praise him, ye heavens of heavens, and ye waters that *be* above the heavens. Let them praise the name of the LORD: for he commanded, and they were created."

God's Heavenly Creations- the Angels:

Before we go on with more details about the creation of the world, there are some other truths that are important to the background of our story. In Psalm 104:1-4, we read that in the beginning, God created special ministering spirits called angels:

Ps 104:1-4 "Bless the LORD, O my soul. O LORD my God, thou art very great; thou art clothed with honour and majesty. Who coverest *thyself* with light as *with* a garment: who stretchest out the heavens like a curtain: Who layeth the beams of his chambers in the waters: who maketh the clouds his chariot: who walketh upon the wings of the wind: Who maketh his angels spirits; his ministers a flaming fire:

When God stretched forth the heavens at the beginning of creation, He also created the angels. Angels are God's messengers who do His bidding. According to the verse we read earlier in Job 38:7, the angels, called "the sons of God," were present at the laying of the foundations of the earth. Since the dawn of creation, the angels have been present as God's special ministering spirits. They play a vital role in the carrying out of God's purpose in the world in which we live, even today.

The Triune God:

Another truth we find introduced in the first chapter of Genesis is that God is a triune God- He is one God, but three Persons -God the Father, God the Son, and God the Holy Spirit. This is seen in the first verses of Genesis 1, where God the Holy Spirit is specifically mentioned as moving upon the face of the waters. In Genesis 1:26, we see this truth again. There God says, "Let us make man in our image..." The "us" refers to the fact that God the Father, God the Son, and God the Holy Spirit were all involved in the work of creation. We know from Genesis 1 that God the Father spoke the world into existence by the word of His mouth. The Bible also tells us that God the Son, Jesus Christ, was involved in every part of the work of creation. In fact, John 1:1-3 tells us that all things were made by Him:

Joh 1:1-3 "In the beginning was the Word, and the Word was with God, and the Word was God. The same was in the beginning with God. All things were made by him; and without him was not any thing made that was made."

The Apostle Paul echoed this same truth in Colossians 1 concerning Jesus Christ, God's Son:

Col 1:16-17 "For by him were all things created, that are in heaven, and that are in earth, visible and invisible, whether *they be* thrones, or dominions, or principalities, or powers: all things were created by him, and for him: And he is before all things, and by him all things consist."

Jesus Christ, God's Son, is the active agent in the creation of all things, and God the Holy Spirit is the life-giving agent in creation:

Ps 104:30 "Thou sendest forth thy spirit, they are created: and thou renewest the face of the earth."

Psalm 104 is an amazing description of God's glory displayed through creation. All three Persons of the Godhead- Father, Son, and Holy Ghost -were active in the creation of the world and the universe. All visible, physical things in creation, as well as the invisible, spiritual things were created by Almighty God. God continues to create life, and He holds the very universe together by the word of His power (Heb. 1:3).

From the first two verses of Genesis and the other passages above, we learn the following truths:

-God laid the foundations of the earth and stretched forth the heavens as the first step to His creative work. He created all things by His power and continues to create life and sustain His creation.

-God created the angels as ministering spirits.

-God is a trinity- one God in three distinct Persons -Father, Son, and Holy Spirit.

The Completion of God's Perfect Creation in Six Literal Days: (Genesis 1:3-31):

Going back to the creation account in Genesis 1, we read that on the first day, God created light:

Ge 1:3-5 "And God said, Let there be light: and there was light. And God saw the light, that *it was* good: and God divided the light from the darkness. And God called the light Day, and the darkness he called Night. And the evening and the morning were the first day."

It is interesting to note that God did not need to create the sun, moon, and stars first in order to make light upon the earth. The Bible tells us that God Himself is light:

1Jo 1:5 "This then is the message which we have heard of him, and declare unto you, that God is light, and in him is no darkness at all."

God is the source of all light, both physical and spiritual. It is through Him that light shined out of the darkness upon the formless earth; and it is through Him that we ourselves can understand and know truth and light of a spiritual nature. There is no light apart from the God of Heaven. Man does not have light in himself, but must come to God for spiritual light.

The perfection of God's work and the creation of time:

Everything that God created was good. When God says something is "good," He speaks from a view of absolute, holy perfection. God's creation was perfectly pleasing to Him. The Bible tells us in Genesis 1:3-5 that the light God made was good. God then divided the light from the darkness. When God divided the light from the darkness, He created day and night. This was the creation of time as we know it. Here we have the plain truth that **God created everything in six literal days.** Each day had an evening and a morning. God created all things by His power. There is no place whatsoever in God's Word for the man-made theory of evolution. For a person of faith in the God of the Bible, God has given us His clear truth. By His power He created the heaven and the earth in six literal days. He is the Almighty God.

On the second day, God created the "firmament"- the atmosphere surrounding the earth. The atmosphere was made from the water of the earth. God called the firmament "heaven":

Ge 1:6-8 "And God said, Let there be a firmament in the midst of the waters, and let it divide the waters from the waters. And God made the firmament, and divided the waters which *were* under the firmament from the waters which *were* above the firmament: and it was so. And God called the firmament Heaven. And the evening and the morning were the second day."

On the third day, God gathered the waters on the earth into seas and made the dry land appear. He created the plants and trees, the grass, herbs, and fruit. He created the trees and plants to be mature and lush to be able to reproduce themselves and to grow fruit from their own seeds:

Ge 1:9-13 "And God said, Let the waters under the heaven be gathered together unto one place, and let the dry *land* appear: and it was so. And God called the dry *land* Earth; and the gathering together of the waters called he Seas: and God saw that *it was* good. And God said, Let the earth bring forth grass, the herb yielding seed, *and* the fruit tree yielding fruit after his kind, whose seed *is* in itself, upon the earth: and it was so. And the earth brought forth grass, *and* herb yielding seed after his kind, and the tree yielding fruit, whose seed *was* in itself, after his kind: and God saw that *it was* good. And the evening and the morning were the third day."

On the fourth day, God made the sun, and the moon, and the stars, and all the host of Heaven. On the fifth day, God made the birds, the sea creatures, and the fish. On the sixth day, God made all the beasts and cattle, and every creeping thing- all of the land animals and insects:

Ge 1:14-25 "And God said, Let there be lights in the firmament of the heaven to divide the day from the night; and let them be for signs, and for seasons, and for days, and years: And let them be for lights in the firmament of the heaven to give light upon the earth: and it was so. And God made two great lights; the greater light to rule the day, and the lesser light to rule the night: *he made* the stars also. And God set them in the firmament of the heaven to give light upon the earth, And to rule over the day and over the night, and to divide the light from the darkness: and God saw that *it was* good. And the evening and the morning were the fourth day. And God said, Let the waters bring forth abundantly the moving creature that hath life, and fowl *that* may fly above the earth in the open firmament of heaven. And God created great whales, and every living creature that moveth, which the waters brought forth abundantly, after their kind, and every winged fowl after his kind: and God saw that *it was* good. And God blessed them, saying, Be fruitful, and multiply, and fill the waters in the seas, and let fowl multiply in the earth. And the evening and the morning were the fifth day. And God said, Let the earth bring forth the living creature after his kind, cattle, and creeping thing, and beast of the earth after his kind: and it was so. And God made the beast of the earth after his kind, and cattle after their kind, and every thing that creepeth upon the earth after his kind: and God saw that *it was* good."

Finally- also on the sixth day -God created man.

<u>*Man: a unique creation:*</u>

Ge 1:26-27 "And God said, Let us make man in our image, after our likeness: and let them have dominion over the fish of the sea, and over the fowl of the air, and

over the cattle, and over all the earth, and over every creeping thing that creepeth upon the earth. So God created man in his *own* image, in the image of God created he him; male and female created he them."

As we mentioned, God is the triune God- God the Father, God the Son, and God the Holy Spirit. God created mankind male and female, and they are very special. They were created in God's image, after His likeness. Like God, mankind has a spiritual aspect and is a trinity made up of a body, a soul, and a spirit:

1 Th 5:23 "And the very God of peace sanctify you wholly; and *I pray God* your whole spirit and soul and body be preserved blameless unto the coming of our Lord Jesus Christ..;"

Heb 4:12 "For the word of God *is* quick, and powerful, and sharper than any twoedged sword, piercing even to the dividing asunder of soul and spirit, and of the joints and marrow, and *is* a discerner of the thoughts and intents of the heart."

The soul and the spirit of man are what make mankind unique. The soul of man is made up of the emotions, the mind, the will, and the personality. Man can make choices concerning good or evil because he has a soul. God gives man a sense of right and wrong in his conscience because he has a soul. The spirit, the most special part of man, is that part that God created to have fellowship with Him. It is the part that reflects God's image. Sadly, as we will learn, the spirit of man died when Adam and Eve sinned against God. Because each person is born with an eternal soul, there will never be a time when they will not exist somewhere. As God is eternal, so is the soul of man. Though a person's body will die, his soul will live on in eternity either in Heaven or in Hell. People, unlike animals, are eternal beings and must answer to their Eternal Creator.

Mankind at the Time of Creation: Innocence: Genesis 2

At the time that Adam and Eve were first created, they were created in innocence and perfection. They were made in God's image with a body, an eternal soul, and a living spirit through which they could have sweet communion with their Creator.

Ge 2:7 "And the LORD God formed man *of* the dust of the ground, and breathed into his nostrils the breath of life; and man became a living soul."

Man and woman in fellowship with God:

As we mentioned, Genesis 1:27 tells us that God created mankind as both male and female. Adam, the man, was made first, then God created the woman, Eve, from Adam's side. Eve was created to be a help "meet for" or suitable for Adam (Ge. 2:18-22). When God completed His creation, He said it was "very good." Everything was perfect and complete. When Adam and Eve were created, they were innocent and pure.

God planted a special garden for the man and the woman to live in. It was full of the beautiful things God made and His abundant blessings. Two special trees were in this garden- the tree of life and the tree of the knowledge of good and evil. God gave Adam and Eve the freedom to enjoy all the trees of the garden except one- the tree of the knowledge of good and evil. Concerning this tree God said, "But of the tree of the knowledge of good and evil, thou shalt not eat of it; for in the day that thou eatest thereof thou shalt surely die" (Ge. 2:17). God gave this one test of obedience to Adam and Eve. We see from this that God created Adam and Eve with **free will**. He gave them the choice to obey or to disobey. Sadly, Adam and Eve chose to disobey God. Their choice would have bitter consequences for all of creation. But God, the great Creator, is also the great Redeemer. His plan and power are glorious for those who put their trust in Him.

"This is My Father's World"

This is my Father's world,
And to my list'ning ears
All nature sings, and round me rings
The music of the spheres.

This is my Father's world:
I rest me in the thought
Of rocks and trees, of skies and seas—
His hand the wonders wrought.

Be An Example

This is my Father's world:
The birds their carols raise,
The morning light, the lily white,
Declare their Maker's praise.

This is my Father's world:
He shines in all that's fair;
In the rustling grass I hear Him pass,
He speaks to me everywhere.

This is my Father's world:
Oh, let me ne'er forget
That though the wrong seems oft so strong,
God is the ruler yet.

This is my Father's world,
The battle is not done:
Jesus who died shall be satisfied,
And earth and Heav'n be one.

-Maltbie D. Babcock, 1901

Chapter 2: "The Life of Abel" (Part 2)

Memory Verse:

Hebrews 11:6 "But without faith *it is* impossible to please *him*: for he that cometh to God must believe that he is, and *that* he is a rewarder of them that diligently seek him."

Scripture Reading: Genesis 3

Key Lessons: Foundational truths concerning God, the nature of mankind, and salvation

Genesis 3 is the record of one of the most tragic days in human history- the day that sin and death entered into the world. We learn from this passage that sin and death entered God's perfect world because of Adam and Eve's own choice. Their choice would affect the destiny of the entire human race. Sin had devastating consequences for all creation. It's important for us to understand how sin is defined according to the Bible. The Bible defines sin as:

Breaking God's commands:

1Jo 3:4 "Whosoever committeth sin transgresseth also the law: for sin is the transgression of the law."

Refusing to do what is right and good:

Jas 4:17 "Therefore to him that knoweth to do good, and doeth *it* not, to him it is sin."

Unrighteousness- actions, attitudes, and thoughts that are wicked in God's sight:

1Jo 5:17 "All unrighteousness is sin..."

Be An Example

The Bible also tells us in Ephesians 2:1-3 that the spirit of man is dead in trespasses and sins- dead to God and to all that is good and right because we are sinners by nature and by choice:

Eph 2:1-3 "And you *hath he quickened*, who were dead in trespasses and sins; Wherein in time past ye walked according to the course of this world, according to the prince of the power of the air, the spirit that now worketh in the children of disobedience: Among whom also we all had our conversation in times past in the lusts of our flesh, fulfilling the desires of the flesh and of the mind; and were by nature the children of wrath, even as others."

Sin separates us from God and keeps us from having a relationship with Him. Only through God's gift of salvation can the spirit of man be made alive again. As we mentioned, God created mankind with a free will. He gave one restriction to Adam and Eve in their beautiful garden home. God told Adam that they were not to eat the fruit of the tree called "the Tree of the Knowledge of Good and Evil." God also told Adam the consequences of disobedience:

Ge 2:16-17 "And the LORD God commanded the man, saying, Of every tree of the garden thou mayest freely eat: But of the tree of the knowledge of good and evil, thou shalt not eat of it: for in the day that thou eatest thereof thou shalt surely die."

God gave Adam His plain truth. Remember, the Bible defines sin as breaking God's commandments. God's command was a test for Adam and his wife, Eve. Eve also knew God's command, as we will see, even though it was given directly to Adam even before she was created. God gave Adam and Eve His truth for their protection. He gave them a free will to choose to obey or to disobey. He told them the grave consequences that would come if they turned from His truth and disobeyed His command. God had given Adam and Eve great blessing and freedom in their garden home. It was up to them to choose to continue in that place of sweet communion with Him through obedience and faith in God's Word.

It is the same for us today. God has given us His plain truth in the Bible. God's Word is available for us to read, to study, and to obey. When we obey God's truth and follow His Word, we have peace, and joy, and blessing. But when we choose to reject God's truth and follow our own way, we will find ourselves in a place of confusion, guilt, sorrow, and separation from fellowship with God. We lose everything that is precious in our relationship with God when we turn from Him and follow our own lusts. God had given Adam and Eve every blessing. What would they do with it? Genesis 3 tells us the sad account of their choice. There was another person that Adam and Eve chose to listen to instead of God.

The Entrance of the Serpent and the Fall of Man: Genesis 3

In Genesis 3, we learn about a creature called the serpent- an earthly creature who became inhabited by a spiritual being named Satan. Satan, originally named Lucifer, was a glorious, angelic creature called a cherub. But sometime after his creation, Lucifer rebelled against God. He decided that he wanted to take God's place. The description of Lucifer's beauty and his fall are found in the following Scriptures:

Eze 28:12-17 "...Thus saith the Lord GOD; Thou sealest up the sum, full of wisdom, and perfect in beauty. Thou hast been in Eden the garden of God; every precious stone *was* thy covering, the sardius, topaz, and the diamond, the beryl, the onyx, and the jasper, the sapphire, the emerald, and the carbuncle, and gold: the workmanship of thy tabrets and of thy pipes was prepared in thee in the day that thou wast created. Thou *art* the anointed cherub that covereth; and I have set thee *so*: thou wast upon the holy mountain of God; thou hast walked up and down in the midst of the stones of fire. Thou *wast* perfect in thy ways from the day that thou wast created, till iniquity was found in thee. By the multitude of thy merchandise they have filled the midst of thee with violence, and thou hast sinned: therefore I will cast thee as profane out of the mountain of God: and I will destroy thee, O covering cherub, from the midst of the stones of fire. Thine heart was lifted up because of thy beauty, thou hast corrupted thy wisdom by reason of thy brightness: I will cast thee to the ground, I will lay thee before kings, that they may behold thee."

Isaiah 14:12-15 "How art thou fallen from heaven, O Lucifer, son of the morning! How art thou cut down to the ground, which didst weaken the nations! For thou hast said in thine heart, I will ascend into heaven, I will exalt my throne above the stars of God: I will sit also upon the mount of the congregation, in the sides of the north: I will ascend above the heights of the clouds; I will be like the most High. Yet thou shalt be brought down to hell, to the sides of the pit."

Through his wicked choice Lucifer became the Devil, or Satan. His goal became the ruin of God's creation, and in particular, the destruction of man who was made in the image of God. In Genesis 3, Satan came to the woman, Eve, in the form of the serpent, a creature the Bible calls "more subtle than any beast of the field the Lord God had made." "Subtle" means "clever." This creature was the perfect instrument for Satan to use to tempt Eve. When we think of a serpent today, we think of a slithering reptile, for that is what the serpent became as a result of God's judgment. But at the time of Genesis 3, the serpent was the most intelligent creature that God had made in the animal world. Satan chose this creature to approach Eve. Coming through the wise serpent, Satan knew his temptation would sound like a sweet deal.

Satan's tactics have not changed. He uses the most attractive hosts he can find to draw people into sin. He makes temptation to do evil sound good and even sensible. Satan packages his temptation in the guise of beauty, fun, and innocence. He often uses people we like or even people who are kind to us to draw us to do things that we know are wrong- things that perhaps our own parents or other godly people in our lives have warned us not to be involved in. Often other young people may give the argument, "Well, you don't need to just believe what your parents tell you to believe, you need to decide for yourself what you want to believe." While it's true that we need to understand why we believe what we do, we also need to trust the wisdom of godly parents and authority, and most of all, the wisdom of the Word of God. Figuring things out on our own is never a good idea. God has given us all the right guidance for life in His Word. That is the place we need to seek answers and truth. When temptation comes, or when someone presents a seemingly plausible doubt concerning what godly parents and teachers or pastors have taught us, we need to ask, "What does God's Word say?" God's truth is to be our shield against temptation (Ps. 91:4) and our guide for choosing what is right (Ps. 119:105). God warns us in the book of Proverbs to be very careful who we listen to. He warns us to hold fast to the teaching of Christian parents and God's Word:

Pr 1:7-10 "The fear of the LORD *is* the beginning of knowledge: *but* fools despise wisdom and instruction. My son, hear the instruction of thy father, and forsake not the law of thy mother: For they *shall be* an ornament of grace unto thy head, and chains about thy neck. My son, if sinners entice thee, consent thou not."

Pr 3:5-7 "Trust in the LORD with all thine heart; and lean not unto thine own understanding. In all thy ways acknowledge him, and he shall direct thy paths. Be not wise in thine own eyes: fear the LORD, and depart from evil."

Unfortunately for Eve, the more she listened to the serpent's enticing words, the more she forgot the commandment of the LORD. The story of how Satan deceived Eve through the serpent is found in Genesis 3:1-6:

Ge 3:1-6 "Now the serpent was more subtil than any beast of the field which the LORD God had made. And he said unto the woman, Yea, hath God said, Ye shall not eat of every tree of the garden? And the woman said unto the serpent, We may eat of the fruit of the trees of the garden: But of the fruit of the tree which *is* in the midst of the garden, God hath said, Ye shall not eat of it, neither shall ye touch it, lest ye die. And the serpent said unto the woman, Ye shall not surely die: For God doth know that in the day ye eat thereof, then your eyes shall be opened, and ye shall be as gods, knowing good and evil. And when the woman saw that the tree *was* good for food, and that it *was* pleasant to the eyes, and a tree to be desired to make *one* wise, she took of the fruit thereof, and did eat, and gave also unto her husband with her; and he did eat."

In this passage, we see the pattern of Satan's temptation:

First, Satan questioned the Word of God and twisted it around a bit - "Hath God said?" In essence he was saying, "Did God really say that?" He planted a doubt in Eve's mind about what God said. Surely He didn't mean it that way? Surely God would not forbid something that is so beautiful and nice. Satan also made God's command sound restrictive and unfair rather than loving and generous: "...Hath God said, Ye shall not eat of every tree of the garden?"

Next, Satan flatly denied God's Word along with the consequences of sin God had promised would come if they disobeyed- "Ye shall not surely die…"

Then, he cast doubt upon the goodness of God- "For God doth know that in the day ye eat thereof, then your eyes shall be opened." Satan made it sound as if God was keeping something good from them, when in reality; God's command protected them from harm.

Finally, Satan appealed to Eve's own pride, "…ye shall be as gods, knowing good and evil." Satan made Eve think that what he offered her was far better than what God would give her; in fact, with the wisdom imparted from this forbidden fruit, she would become like a god herself. That was the clincher for Eve.

Tragically, Eve listened to Satan as he spoke to her through that crafty serpent. Genesis 3:6 tells us that she "saw that the tree was good for food, and that it was pleasant to the eyes, and a tree to be desired to make one wise." Satan's deception worked, and Eve's own lust for the thing that God had forbidden drew her to partake of the fruit (*Lust is an insatiable desire for something outside the bounds that God has set for our good and for our safety*). Satan's work was done.

When Eve turned her longing gaze to that tree, what God had said no longer mattered. All that mattered was fulfilling her desire for the fruit of that tree and gaining the wisdom that the serpent had promised. She took and ate of the tree that God had clearly commanded them not to eat from "and gave also to her husband with her; and he did eat." Genesis 3:6 tells us that Adam was there with his wife, but he did not stop Eve from disobeying God's command. Genesis 3:17 says that Adam listened to his wife instead of to God. The results were disastrous.

Satan has not changed his ways. He uses the same tactics in his temptations today -casting doubt upon God's Word, twisting God's Word, and denying God's Word. He appeals to "the lust of the flesh, the lust of the eyes, and the pride of life" (1 Jo. 2:16).

The Wages of Sin: Death:

In his temptation, Satan convinced Eve that God didn't really mean what He said. He deceived her into believing that she would not die, but rather that she and Adam would "be as gods, knowing good and evil." But when Adam and Eve took of the fruit of that forbidden tree, death came upon them just as God said it would. You may say, but they did not drop dead when they ate of the fruit, so how did they die? To understand the reality of what happened to Adam and Eve, we must understand the meaning of death. Death in the Bible means **separation,** and it has three different aspects: physical, spiritual, and eternal:

Physical death: When a person's body dies, the soul separates from the body and goes to one of two destinations- Heaven, the abode of God, or Hell, a place of eternal fire and eternal separation from God. A literal description of what happens at death is found in a story the Lord Jesus Christ told in Luke 16:

Lu 16:19-23 "There was a certain rich man, which was clothed in purple and fine linen, and fared sumptuously every day: And there was a certain beggar named Lazarus, which was laid at his gate, full of sores, And desiring to be fed with the crumbs which fell from the rich man's table: moreover the dogs came and licked his sores. And it came to pass, that the beggar died, and was carried by the angels into Abraham's bosom: the rich man also died, and was buried; And in hell he lift up his eyes, being in torments..."

Jesus told this story to give us a literal picture of what happens to the soul at death. This account was a true story, witnessed by Jesus Christ, the Son of God. Only He who inhabits eternity and sees even the hidden things of the spiritual world beyond this life could tell this story from the perspective of an eyewitness. Christ stated this story as fact, for He gave the name of the man of faith- Lazarus- as one precious and known to Him. The contrast between the men was clear -one had faith in God and His truth- Lazarus, the beggar; the other- the rich man -had refused God's way and ended up in hell. When the separation of the soul from the body occurred at death, Lazarus' was carried by the angels to "Abraham's bosom"- the place God had prepared for those who trust in Him. The Bible says that Abraham was a man who believed God, and "it was counted unto him for righteousness" (Ro. 4:3). This is the only way that anyone gets to Heaven- by faith in God and His truth. The rich man's soul went to the torments of hell. He didn't go there because he was rich. He went there because of unbelief. It is refusing to trust God's truth that sends people to hell. This man's riches, however, are a picture for us of what he lived for and trusted in. He lived for this world and its pleasures, and had no concern for the truth of God and the life to come. He may have been religious, like the men Jesus was preaching to, but his trust was in his own way. Lazarus was poor in this world, but his trust was in God. His hope was in eternity. It is interesting to note that Christ named the man who had put his trust in God, but the man who had refused God was nameless, just as all who reject Christ will one day be nameless before God (Mt. 7:21-23). To them Christ will say, "I never knew you."

In this account, Jesus was making a point to the self-righteous leaders of His day. He was letting them know that their religion would not save them. They were wicked sinners and religious hypocrites who rejected Jesus Christ. They were headed to the same eternal torment as the rich man Christ had described. This true story from the Word of God shows us what happens to a soul at death. What we do with Jesus Christ and His truth makes all the difference.

Spiritual death: Spiritual death is spiritual separation from God. When Adam and Eve sinned against God, the spirit within them -that part of man that God had created to have a relationship with Him died instantly. Sin destroyed their relationship with God and separated them from fellowship with Him. They were spiritually dead to the God they once knew and loved and enslaved to Satan -the god they had chosen.

When Adam and Eve sinned, they no longer had sweet communion with God. Instead of a Heavenly Father, God became a fearful Judge. Adam and Eve no longer looked forward to God's presence, but hid from Him in fear and tried to cover their sin. Perhaps you have experienced something of this feeling in your own life when you engaged in some secret sin or disobeyed your parents or some other authority. What was once sweet fellowship and friendship became fearful dread of discovery and punishment. Adam and Eve had this feeling for the first time after they chose to sin.

When they followed Satan, Adam and Eve became his subjects and his children. Satan is a cruel taskmaster. Because of their choice, all of Adam and Eve's offspring- the entire human race -are sinners. David, the sweet psalmist of Israel, spoke of this truth when he said in Psalm 51:5, "Behold, I was shapen in iniquity; and in sin did my mother conceive me." We are born sinners. The Bible says that without God's salvation, all of us are spiritually dead in trespasses and sins (Eph. 2:1). This was the instant death that Adam and Eve experienced when they disobeyed God.

Eternal death: The final type of death is eternal death. Eternal death is eternal separation from God in hell. Every sinner who dies physically without trusting God's way of salvation will be eternally separated from God in hell -a place of everlasting fire. Spiritual separation from God does not end with physical death. It goes on into eternity in a place called Hell and, eventually, in a place called the lake of fire -the place of ultimate judgment for Satan and all who follow him. The Bible calls this the second death (Re. 20:14). Hell was not created for human beings. Hell was created as the place of eternal judgment for the Devil and his angels (Mt. 25:41). When Lucifer rebelled against God and became Satan, some of the other heavenly angels chose to follow Lucifer instead of God. These fallen angels now belong to Satan's dark realm (Eph. 6:12; Jude 1:6). But when Adam and Eve chose to listen to Satan instead of to God, Satan's destiny became their destiny, along with all of Adam's offspring. Without God's intervention, they, like the angels that followed the Devil, were doomed to eternal death.

Genesis 3:7-10 tells the sad consequences of spiritual death that happened the moment that Adam and Eve sinned against God:

Ge 3:7-10 "And the eyes of them both were opened, and they knew that they *were* naked; and they sewed fig leaves together, and made themselves aprons. And they heard the voice of the LORD God walking in the garden in the cool of the day: and Adam and his wife hid themselves from the presence of the LORD God amongst the trees of the garden. And the LORD God called unto Adam, and said unto him, Where *art* thou? And he said, I heard thy voice in the garden, and I was afraid, because I *was* naked; and I hid myself."

Adam and Eve knew instantly that they were naked before God. Before they sinned, the Bible tells us that "they were both naked, man and his wife, and were not ashamed" (Ge. 2:25). They were innocent and pure before God until they disobeyed. They had nothing to hide. But when they chose to disobey, they felt guilt and shame for the first time. They were no longer clean before God. They were naked and ashamed. They tried to cover their shame and nakedness by sewing together aprons made from fig leaves. It was a useless effort and a picture of how man from then on would try to cover his own sin by works that fall miserably short of God's perfect standard. All of Adam and Eve's efforts could never hide their sin or undo what they had done.

Have you ever done something you knew was wrong, and then tried to hide it? Have you ever felt the misery and fear of knowing you will be found out? This is the awfulness of sin. None of us can hide from God. Everything we do, every sin we commit is open to His sight:

Heb 4:13 "Neither is there any creature that is not manifest in his sight: but all things *are* naked and opened unto the eyes of him with whom we have to do."

Pr 28:13 "He that covereth his sins shall not prosper: but whoso confesseth and forsaketh *them* shall have mercy."

When Adam and Eve heard God walking in the garden, they no longer looked forward to being in His presence. Instead, they tried to hide from the LORD. God's presence was not sweet to them, but fearful. Never before had they known guilt, and fear, and the dread of judgment; but these were the instant results of sin- the first sensations of spiritual death. Adam and Eve were separated from God for the first time. The sweet relationship they once had with God was broken, and it was completely their fault.

God Seeks Sinners:

As the LORD God walked in the garden in the cool of the day, He called to Adam. He knew what Adam and Eve had done. God's call to Adam shows us a precious truth about God. Even though Adam and Eve had sinned against Him, God sought them out. God seeks sinners and longs to save them from their sin.

He called to Adam and said, "Where *art* thou?" God did not leave Adam and Eve to die in their sin. He called them to repentance, just as He does each one of us.

When God confronted Adam, the truth came out:

Ge 3:11-14 "And he said, Who told thee that thou *wast* naked? Hast thou eaten of the tree, whereof I commanded thee that thou shouldest not eat? And the man said, The woman whom thou gavest *to be* with me, she gave me of the tree, and I did eat. And the LORD God said unto the woman, What *is* this *that* thou hast done? And the woman said, The serpent beguiled me, and I did eat. And the LORD God said unto the serpent, Because thou hast done this, thou *art* cursed above all cattle, and above every beast of the field; upon thy belly shalt thou go, and dust shalt thou eat all the days of thy life:"

Sin had an effect on all of Adam and Eve's relationships. Never before had they known a break in sweet fellowship with each other, but sin brought that too. Sin tainted their love for one another. Adam tried to blame Eve for his sin, and Eve blamed the serpent. They didn't want to take responsibility for what they had done. They made excuses for their sin, and then turned on each other. All of this misery came upon them because they sinned against God. They were separated from God, and their own love for one other was marred by sin.

The moment they sinned, another kind of death came into Adam and Eve's world. They came under the certain sentence of physical death. They were going to die. In the process of death, they would experience sickness, pain, and weakness -things they had never known before. They would know the sorrow, misery, and separation that would come with the death of loved ones. God told Adam in Genesis 3:19: "...for dust thou *art*, and unto dust shalt thou return." Physical death hung over them from that moment on and did its gradual work in their bodies. The sentence of death and judgment hung over their lives like a foreboding cloud:

Heb 9:27 "And as it is appointed unto men once to die, but after this the judgment:"

In this verse we find the most fearful sentence that hung over Adam and Eve and all of their descendants - the judgment of God that will come upon each and every soul of Adam's race. Because of sin, Adam and Eve had the sentence of eternal death upon them:

Ro 6:23 "For the wages of sin *is* death;"

Sin's penalty is eternal. Sinners can never pay it or atone for it. No good deeds can erase sin, and no good deeds can reform man's sinful nature. No religious ritual can cleanse a person from sin. All of Adam's seed are marked with sin's curse. We are born with a nature to sin, and we sin by choice. As a result, the awful penalty of eternal death is upon the entire human race:

Ro 5:12 "Wherefore, as by one man sin entered into the world, and death by sin; and so death passed upon all men, for that all have sinned:"

God Provides Salvation for Sinners:

Every child born of man is born a sinner with the sentence of death- both physical and spiritual -upon him or her. In fact, man's sin cursed all of God's creation with sorrow and death. No more could God say His creation was very good. Man had ruined it. By his choice he had plunged the whole world into groaning and misery (Ro. 8:20-22). Now, as part of the curse, the earth would produce thorns and thistles. Heartache, toil, pain, and death touched everything. Everything in nature that has life in it has death in it as well. Trees and flowers die. Animals die. And man dies. This was the result of Adam and Eve's choice. But though Abel's parents made that terrible choice, God in mercy, had a plan to save mankind from eternal death for those who will receive it. God would send a Savior, to provide forgiveness and eternal life for those who will put their faith in Him. Only the sinless, eternal God could pay the eternal price for man's sin. He would do it by coming Himself, in the person of His Son, Jesus Christ, to die in the place of sinners. God's first promise of the Savior is found in Genesis 3:15. God gave this wondrous promise immediately after Adam and Eve sinned against Him. In love, God had already provided a way to save them from the eternal death sentence that hung over them:

Ge 3:14-15 "And the LORD God said unto the serpent, Because thou hast done this, thou *art* cursed above all cattle, and above every beast of the field; upon thy belly shalt thou go, and dust shalt thou eat all the days of thy life: And I will put enmity between thee and the woman, and between thy seed and her seed; it shall bruise thy head, and thou shalt bruise his heel."

In this passage, God promised, that though the serpent had beguiled Eve to sin, God would send One, the Seed of the woman, who would bruise the head of the serpent. The physical creature that Satan had inhabited- the serpent - was cursed to crawl on his belly from that time on. The spiritual serpent, Satan, would one day be defeated by the promised Seed of the woman. This Seed of the woman God promised was none other than Jesus Christ, the sinless Son of God, who would be born of a virgin, and would bruise Satan's head with a deadly wound when He died on a cross and pay the eternal penalty for man's sin. Satan would bruise Christ's heel when Jesus died on the cross of Calvary; but Christ would defeat Satan by paying the penalty of sin for sinners like Adam and Eve. Christ would provide salvation for sinners from eternal death in hell and give them a relationship with God again through faith in His Son. This is God's promise for all who will accept the salvation He would provide through His Son:

Joh 1:12 "But as many as received him, to them gave he power to become the sons of God, *even* to them that believe on his name:"

God gave Adam and Eve this promise even before He talked to them about the other consequences of their sin. God was holding out the hope of salvation to them- and to all of us -from the very beginning.

The Earthly Consequences of Sin

Sadly, there would be more consequences of sin for Adam and Eve, even in daily life:

Ge 3:16-19 "Unto the woman he said, I will greatly multiply thy sorrow and thy conception; in sorrow thou shalt bring forth children; and thy desire *shall be* to thy husband, and he shall rule over thee. And unto Adam he said, Because thou hast hearkened unto the voice of thy wife, and hast eaten of the tree, of which I commanded thee, saying, Thou shalt not eat of it: cursed *is* the ground for thy sake; in sorrow shalt thou eat *of* it all the days of thy life; Thorns also and thistles shall it bring forth to thee; and thou shalt eat the herb of the field; In the sweat of thy face shalt thou eat bread, till thou return unto the ground; for out of it wast thou taken: for dust thou *art*, and unto dust shalt thou return."

For the woman, there would be increased conception and sorrow in bringing forth children. She would also be subject to the rule of her husband. For the man, thorns, thistles, and cursed ground would make his work very difficult. In sorrow and toil Adam would have to work to survive and to provide food for himself and for his family. Finally, at the end, there would be the sorrow of physical death for Adam and Eve and for all of their offspring.

Adam and Eve's Faith and God's Picture of Salvation:

There was no turning back now. The consequences of sin were certain. But God's promise of a Savior was sure as well. After God gave Adam and Eve the promise of the Savior to come, the Bible says in Genesis 3:20, that "Adam called his wife's name Eve; because she was the mother of all living." In the naming of his wife, Adam demonstrated his faith that what God had said concerning their future and His promise of salvation was true. God would send the Savior, and Eve would be the mother of the entire human race. God was not finished with Adam and Eve. He had a plan for their salvation and for the salvation of all who would believe His promise. God then gave Adam and Eve a picture of the salvation that He would provide through the shed blood of the Savior. Genesis 3:21 tells us:

Ge 3:21 "Unto Adam also and to his wife did the LORD God make coats of skins, and clothed them."

To make these coats of skins for Adam and Eve, God had to shed the blood of innocent animals. The death of these animals was a picture of the fact that the penalty for sin is death. No animal had ever died before sin entered the world. These animals had to die to provide a covering for the nakedness of Adam and Eve. This pointed to the fact that one day the sinless Son of God- the Lamb of God (Joh. 1:29) -would shed His blood upon a cross and die in the place of sinners

(Ro. 6:23). Jesus Christ would pay the penalty of sin for all. Those who accept His sacrifice as the only payment for their salvation and believe that He was buried and rose again from the dead receive forgiveness and eternal life. This is God's gift of salvation. God gave Adam and Eve a picture of that gift when He clothed them that day. Through the shed blood and the skins provided by the animals sacrificed, God demonstrated a picture of Christ's blood that cleanses us from sin. When He made coverings for Adam and Eve's nakedness, He pictured the righteousness of Christ that clothes the forgiven sinner and makes him or her righteous before God.

The fact that the coats were made by God demonstrates that God alone can take away sin and provide salvation. Adam and Eve could not cleanse away their sin or please God with their own works. All of Adam and Eve's efforts to cover their sin had failed miserably. That is true for each one of us. We can never take away our own sin or please God with our own works. Everything we do is tainted by sin (Ro. 3:23; Isa. 64:6). **God's way of salvation is the only way.** Those who accept God's salvation by faith are eternally saved <u>by His power alone</u>. Adam and Eve accepted God's covering and believed God's promise of the Savior to come. ***Their worship of God from that day forward was to be God's way and was to picture the truth of God's salvation through the shed blood of the Savior.** As we will see, faith and obedience to God's way would make all the difference in their son, Abel's, life.

Sadly, Adam and Eve could no longer live in the beautiful Garden of Eden. Though forgiven, they were no longer innocent and pure. They could not eat the fruit of the tree of life and live forever as fallen sinners. God drove them out of the garden to begin life in the world they had chosen -a world cursed by sin:

Ge 3:22-24 "And the LORD God said, Behold, the man is become as one of us, to know good and evil: and now, lest he put forth his hand, and take also of the tree of life, and eat, and live for ever: Therefore the LORD God sent him forth from the garden of Eden, to till the ground from whence he was taken. So he drove out the man; and he placed at the east of the garden of Eden Cherubims, and a flaming sword which turned every way, to keep the way of the tree of life."

Though God drove them out of the garden, He did not leave Adam and Eve without hope. He gave them His promise of salvation through the Savior to come; and He gave His care, strength, and wisdom for the hard days ahead.

From the very beginning, **God provided the way of salvation through faith in His promise**. This life of faith is the key to pleasing God. It was a life of faith in God and His truth that made all the difference in the lives of the people we will discuss in this book. Our memory verse, Hebrews 11:6, explains it this way:

Heb 11:6 "But without faith *it is* impossible to please *him*: for he that cometh to God must believe that he is, and *that* he is a rewarder of them that diligently seek him."

A life of godliness begins with belief in the fact that God **is-** He exists, and He is God. He is the God He claims Himself to be in the Bible- Almighty God, the Creator. He is the only God who can provide salvation to lost sinners. When we come to Him by faith for salvation, He gives us His free gift. There is another part to the verse we read earlier in Romans 6:23 that gives hope for every sinner:

Ro 6:23 "For the wages of sin *is* death; **but** the gift of God *is* eternal life through Jesus Christ our Lord."

God offers His free gift of eternal life to those who will trust in Him and believe His truth! I pray you have received God's gift of eternal life through Jesus Christ our Lord. If not, you can today. God longs to give you His gift of salvation:

Joh 3:16 "For God so loved the world, that he gave his only begotten Son, that whosoever believeth in him should not perish, but have everlasting life."

Ro 5:8-9 "But God commendeth his love toward us, in that, while we were yet sinners, Christ died for us. Much more then, being now justified by his blood, we shall be saved from wrath through him."

Though Abel's parents, sinned grievously against the LORD, God provided a way for their cleansing and redemption through faith in Jesus Christ. This is the way of salvation and the way of daily cleansing for Christians as well. Christ's precious blood still cleanses us from all sin when we come to Him with humble confession:

1Jo 1:7-9 "But if we walk in the light, as he is in the light, we have fellowship one with another, and the blood of Jesus Christ his Son cleanseth us from all sin. If we say that we have no sin, we deceive ourselves, and the truth is not in us. If we confess our sins, he is faithful and just to forgive us *our* sins, and to cleanse us from all unrighteousness."

"Blessed be the Fountain"

Blessed be the fountain of blood,
To a world of sinners revealed;
Blessed be the dear Son of God—
Only by His stripes we are healed.
Though I've wandered far from His fold,
Bringing to my heart pain and woe,
Wash me in the blood of the Lamb,
And I shall be whiter than snow.

Refrain:
Whiter than the snow,
Whiter than the snow;
Wash me in the blood of the Lamb,
And I shall be whiter than snow.

Thorny was the crown that He wore,
And the cross His body o'ercame;
Grievous were the sorrows He bore,
But He suffered thus not in vain.
May I to that fountain be led,
Made to cleanse my sins here below;
Wash me in the blood that He shed,
And I shall be whiter than snow.

Father, I have wandered from Thee,
Often has my heart gone astray;
Crimson do my sins seem to me—
Water cannot wash them away.

Be An Example

Jesus, to that fountain of Thine,
Leaning on Thy promise, I go;
Cleanse me by Thy washing divine,
And I shall be whiter than snow.

-Eden R. Latta, pub.1875

Chapter 3: "The Life of Abel" (Part 3)

Memory Verse:

Heb 11:4 "By faith Abel offered unto God a more excellent sacrifice than Cain, by which he obtained witness that he was righteous, God testifying of his gifts: and by it he being dead yet speaketh."

Scripture Reading: Genesis 4

Key Lessons: Salvation by faith in God's Word; The eternal reward of faith and obedience

God's Blessing upon Adam and Eve:

Ge 4:1-2 "And Adam knew Eve his wife; and she conceived, and bare Cain, and said, I have gotten a man from the LORD. And she again bare his brother Abel. And Abel was a keeper of sheep, but Cain was a tiller of the ground."

Eve knew the LORD had kept His word by giving her strength to bare a son. She said, "I have gotten a man from the LORD" (Gen. 4:1). She saw her children as a gift from God. God gave Adam and Eve two sons, Cain and Abel. Cain was a tiller of the ground- a farmer. Abel was a keeper of sheep- a shepherd.

A Time of Decision for Cain and Abel:

Ge 4:3-4 "And in process of time it came to pass, that Cain brought of the fruit of the ground an offering unto the LORD. And Abel, he also brought of the firstlings of his flock and of the fat thereof."

The time came when the boys were old enough to bring an offering to God. The fact that the boys each came to worship the LORD shows us that salvation is a personal decision. Certainly Cain and Abel had worshipped God with their parents as they were growing up; but the day came when they were old enough to decide personally whether to submit to God's way or to go their own way. Each of us must make that same decision. Adam and Eve could not decide for Cain and Abel. The boys each had to face the decision of whether they would follow God or not.

God's Response to Cain and Abel and their Offerings:

Ge 4: 4-5 "...And the LORD had respect unto Abel and to his offering: But unto Cain and to his offering he had not respect. And Cain was very wroth, and his countenance fell."

We read that God had respect for Abel and to his offering, but not for Cain and his offering. What made the difference? First, let's consider Cain's offering:

Cain's offering: An offering of self will and human works:

When Cain, Adam and Eve's oldest son, came to worship God, he brought "of the fruit of the ground." This was not God's prescribed sacrifice, but rather, an offering of Cain's own work, of his own pride. He had tilled the thorny ground and worked to get the fruit. He knew God's prescribed offering was to be of shed blood- the way taught by the LORD and certainly demonstrated by his parents. The fact that Cain knew the proper offering is shown in God's later conversation with him in Genesis 4:7, "If thou doest well, shalt thou not be accepted?" Cain knew God's way, but he thought his way was better. Genesis 4:5 tells us that God had no respect for Cain's offering. It was an offering of rebellion against God's truth, and God would not accept it.

Abel's offering: An offering of submission and faith:

Abel's offering was different. It showed that he was a young man of faith who accepted God's way of salvation:

Ge 4:4 "And Abel, he also brought of the firstlings of his flock and of the fat thereof."

Abel's offering was exactly what God had commanded. It was an offering of faith and obedience. It was an innocent lamb- a picture of the sinless Lamb of God who would one day offer Himself to die for sinners and shed His blood for the salvation of the world (Jo 3:16; 1 Joh. 2:2).

It is clear that God had given instructions concerning the offerings brought to Him. This is shown by the fact that God accepted Abel's offering. It was not an offering imagined by man. It was an offering directed by God. That God had given these directions is also shown by God's instructions given later in the Old

Testament sacrifices of Israel. God's instructions to Israel exactly match the details of Abel's acceptable sacrifice: the offerings of Israel were to be perfect- without blemish; the fat of the offerings belonged to the Lord (Ex. 12:5; Le. 3:16); and the sacrifices were to be the "firstlings" (Ex. 13:12), or the first born, of the flocks. Abel, in humble, obedient worship, brought the very best to the LORD, but not what he decided was best- he brought what God said was best. Abel's obedience to God's way showed his faith in God's truth. He believed God's way of salvation was right and accepted it for himself, personally. Abel was an example of one who believed God and received God's way of salvation by faith.

The Sad Example of Cain and the First Murder:

When God did not have respect for Cain's offering, the Bible tells us that "Cain was very wroth, and his countenance fell." Cain was angry that God would accept Abel's offering, but not his. Rather than repenting of his disobedience, Cain became furious, and his "countenance fell." He became sullen and rebellious- bitter against God and against his godly brother. Yet, we see here a wondrous truth about the LORD. God, in mercy, loves sinners and seeks their salvation. The Bible tells us in 2Peter 3:9 that God "...is not willing that any should perish, but that all should come to repentance." We see God's great love in the way that He dealt with Cain. In Genesis 3:6-7, God called to Cain:

Ge 4:6-7 "And the LORD said unto Cain, Why art thou wroth? and why is thy countenance fallen? If thou doest well, shalt thou not be accepted? and if thou doest not well, sin lieth at the door. And unto thee *shall be* his desire, and thou shalt rule over him."

God was calling Cain to repent and do what was right while there was still time. Cain had no excuse. He knew God's way. God warned him that if he chose his own way, sin would conquer him. In the end, Cain would become the devil's prey. Sadly, Cain did not listen to God.

Ge 4:8 "And Cain talked with Abel his brother: and it came to pass, when they were in the field, that Cain rose up against Abel his brother, and slew him."

It is an infinite sadness that Cain, rather than responding to God's call, became the first murderer in human history. He rose up against his own brother and brutally killed him. He rebelled against God and rejected God's way of salvation.

In his heart, Cain, like the devil he followed, hated his brother because his brother loved God and did what was right. God confronted Cain again:

Ge 4:9-15 "And the LORD said unto Cain, Where *is* Abel thy brother? And he said, I know not: *Am* I my brother's keeper? And he said, What hast thou done? the voice of thy brother's blood crieth unto me from the ground. And now *art* thou cursed from the earth, which hath opened her mouth to receive thy brother's blood from thy hand; When thou tillest the ground, it shall not henceforth yield unto thee her strength; a fugitive and a vagabond shalt thou be in the earth. And Cain said unto the LORD, My punishment *is* greater than I can bear. Behold, thou hast driven me out this day from the face of the earth; and from thy face shall I be hid; and I shall be a fugitive and a vagabond in the earth; and it shall come to pass, *that* every one that findeth me shall slay me. And the LORD said unto him, Therefore whosoever slayeth Cain, vengeance shall be taken on him sevenfold. And the LORD set a mark upon Cain, lest any finding him should kill him."

Cain could not hide his sin from God. God knew all about it. When God questioned Cain concerning his brother, Cain lied and pretended to know nothing about it. When God pronounced His just judgment upon Cain, Cain still showed no remorse or sorrow for murdering his brother. He only complained that the punishment of God was too harsh. God could have killed Cain outright for what he had done, but instead, He mercifully allowed him to live. He protected him from man's vengeance by placing a mark upon him. Cain became a living example of a rebellious man who rejects the way of God even in the face of God's mercy. Cain did not repent, but Genesis 4:16 tells us:

Ge 4:16 "And Cain went out from the presence of the LORD, and dwelt in the land of Nod, on the east of Eden."

What a sad statement- "Cain went out from the presence of the LORD." He turned his back upon God and chose to live lost and separated from God. He went out and built a city for his own glory, named after his son (Ge. 4:17). Hundreds of years later, all of Cain's descendants- every one of them -perished in the worldwide flood of God's judgment. Many years later, Jesus Christ spoke of men, like Cain, who choose to live for themselves, rather than God:

Mt 16:26-27 "For what is a man profited, if he shall gain the whole world, and lose his own soul? or what shall a man give in exchange for his soul?"

Cain rejected God and lost his soul to eternity in hell. His descendants had many accomplishments in this world, but were eternally destroyed. The book of 1 John tells us the true heart of Cain:

1 Jo 3:12 "Not as Cain, *who* was of that wicked one, and slew his brother. And wherefore slew he him? Because his own works were evil, and his brother's righteous."

Cain was "of that wicked one." That wicked one is Satan. Cain belonged to Satan because he refused God's salvation. Cain was spiritually dead- separated from God by his rebellion and sin. He followed his own religion, and he was a murderer and a liar, just like Satan. Cain was like the self-righteous Pharisees in Christ's day:

Joh 8:44 "Ye are of *your* father the devil, and the lusts of your father ye will do. He was a murderer from the beginning, and abode not in the truth, because there is no truth in him. When he speaketh a lie, he speaketh of his own: for he is a liar, and the father of it."

Cain knew the truth, but he rejected it- like the devil (Satan), he abode not in the truth. Cain murdered Abel because his own works were evil, and his brother's were righteous. He became an example of all those who persecute and murder the godly because of their own rebellious rejection of God. Cain's end was a tragic one. But, you might say, what about Abel? He was killed. How could that be a good end? How was that less tragic than Cain's life? At least Cain got to live a long time on the earth, right?

To understand the blessing and reward of Abel's life, we must see it from God's eternal perspective. What was Abel's reward for going God's way?

The Blessed Example of Abel:

Abel was accepted by God and gained eternal life:

When Abel submitted himself to God's way of salvation, God "had respect unto Abel and to his offering." Abel's faith made him righteous before God. His true faith was shown by his right sacrifice:

Be An Example

Heb 11:4 "By faith Abel offered unto God a more excellent sacrifice than Cain, by which he obtained witness that he was righteous, God testifying of his gifts: and by it he being dead yet speaketh."

Remember our memory verse- Hebrews 11:6, "But without faith *it is* impossible to please *him:* for he that cometh to God must believe that he is, and *that* he is a rewarder of them that diligently seek him." Abel believed God and received the greatest reward possible- eternal life.

Abel suffered persecution and death at the hands of his wicked brother, but his life was not wasted. His soul went to live eternally with God, and his obedience left an example of what true faith in God looks like. Abel was the first person to be faithful to God even unto death. He was God's first martyr and a pattern for suffering Christians of every generation to follow. The Bible tells us that there is a special reward for those who remain faithful to God even in the face of death:

Re 2:10 "Fear none of those things which thou shalt suffer: behold, the devil shall cast *some* of you into prison, that ye may be tried; and ye shall have tribulation ten days: be thou faithful unto death, and I will give thee a crown of life."

Jas 1:12 "Blessed *is* the man that endureth temptation: for when he is tried, he shall receive the crown of life, which the Lord hath promised to them that love him."

Cain lived for this world and lost his soul to eternity in hell. He is in hell today suffering eternal, conscious torment. Hell is forever. Cain's suffering will never end because sin's debt can never be paid by any price except the blood of the Lord Jesus Christ, the Savior. Cain refused God's atonement for his sin. His life in this world was a mere vapor compared to eternity (Jas. 4:14). He will spend an endless eternity in the lake of fire with the devil and his angels (Mt. 25:41) because of his choice to turn away from God and His truth. Abel, on the other hand, suffered for a short time on earth, but gained eternity in Heaven and a reward from God that will never fade away.

<u>*Abel received the praise of his Savior:*</u>

Abel was commended by Jesus Christ Himself as a prophet of God and a righteous man:

Mt 23:34-35 "Wherefore, behold, I send unto you prophets, and wise men, and scribes: and *some* of them ye shall kill and crucify; and *some* of them shall ye scourge in your synagogues, and persecute *them* from city to city: That upon you may come all the righteous blood shed upon the earth, from the blood of righteous Abel unto the blood of Zacharias son of Barachias, whom ye slew between the temple and the altar."

Lu 11:50-51 "That the blood of all the prophets, which was shed from the foundation of the world, may be required of this generation; From the blood of Abel unto the blood of Zacharias, which perished between the altar and the temple: verily I say unto you, It shall be required of this generation."

In these passages, Abel is called both righteous and a prophet (one who speaks forth the truth of God's Word) by the Lord Jesus Christ. What greater reward could Abel receive than the praise of His Savior? This was Abel's crowning achievement- the mark of a life well lived. Abel believed God's Word and was not afraid to speak of the Lord and His truth. He was faithful to God even unto death, and he died for righteousness' sake. What a testimony of courage and faith!

Abel's life of faith still declares God's message of salvation:

Hebrews 11:4 also testifies to the fact that Abel's testimony still lives on:

Heb 11:4 "By faith Abel offered unto God a more excellent sacrifice than Cain, by which he obtained witness that he was righteous, God testifying of his gifts: <u>and by it he being dead yet speaketh.</u>"

By the sacrifice he offered, Abel showed his faith and was declared righteous. God testified that Abel's sacrifice- his gift -was right. His sacrifice pictured the work of Christ just as God had commanded. That example of faith still speaks to us today. We have Abel's story of a faithful life in the Word of God to share even today. Abel's testimony still sounds forth as an example of true faith, salvation in Christ, and humble worship for every person in every generation.

If we could ask him today, "Abel, was it worth it to believe God? Was it worth it to obey God and go his way even when it meant being hated by your own brother? Was it worth it to stand with God even when it meant death?" He would certainly answer "Yes! It was worth it all." Abel is enjoying the eternal reward of

Be An Example

Heaven with his Savior, and his testimony still speaks to every generation of the reward of a life of faith in God.

<u>**Personal Reflection:**</u>

How about you? Like Abel, have you accepted God's way of salvation by faith? God offers it as a free gift to all who will come to Him and receive it. Without salvation, we can never be godly examples. Without salvation, we are spiritually dead- separated from God. We must have a spiritual rebirth. That dead spirit within us must be made new and alive again through faith in Christ if we are ever to have a relationship with God. That is what it means to be "born again."

If you have accepted God's way of salvation, are you living to please the Lord as Abel did? Do you spend time learning about God each day by reading His Word and talking to Him in prayer? Are you willing to speak for Him and share His salvation with others? Will you stand for God and His truth even though you may be hated and criticized? God can give us strength to serve Him and to stand for Him just as Abel did. It will be worth it all to see our Savior and to hear Him say, "Well done, good and faithful servant."

"Saved By Grace"

Someday the silver cord will break,
And I no more as now shall sing;
But, oh, the joy when I shall wake
Within the palace of the King!

Refrain:
And I shall see Him face to face,
And tell the story—Saved by grace.
And I shall see Him face to face,
And tell the story—Saved by grace.

Someday my earthly house will fall;
I cannot tell how soon 'twill be;
But this I know—my All in All
Has now a place in heav'n for me.

Someday, when fades the golden sun

Beneath the rosy tinted west,
My blessed Lord will say, "Well done!"
And I shall enter into rest.

Someday —till then I'll watch and wait,
My lamp all trimmed and burning bright,
That when my Savior opens the gate,
My soul to Him may take its flight.

- Frances J. Crosby, 1891

Be An Example

Chapter 4: "The Life of Isaac" (Part 1)

Memory Verses:

Heb 11:1 "Now faith is the substance of things hoped for, the evidence of things not seen."

Heb 11:8 "By faith Abraham, when he was called to go out into a place which he should after receive for an inheritance, obeyed; and he went out, not knowing whither he went."

Pr 3:5-6 "Trust in the LORD with all thine heart; and lean not unto thine own understanding. In all thy ways acknowledge him, and he shall direct thy paths."

Scripture Reading: Genesis 11-12

Key Lessons: Obedience and Faith

True faith is shown when we trust and obey God even when we can't see- or sometimes even understand -the outcome. We do what God says even when it means doing it alone. We follow God step by step when we cannot see the future. This was the faith of Abraham, the father of a young man named, Isaac. Isaac's parents, Abraham and Sarah, had great faith in the living God. They lived in a city where everyone around them worshipped false gods; yet they chose to leave all they knew to follow the God of Heaven. God chose Abraham out of the idolatrous land of Ur of the Chaldees to be the father of the nation of Israel. It was through this nation that God would send the promised Savior, the Lord Jesus Christ.

To understand where Isaac and his parents came from, let's consider some background about them. If we go back to the time of Adam and Eve, the first man and woman, we read that the Lord gave Adam and Eve a son named Seth after their son Abel was murdered by Cain. When Seth was born, Eve said, "God hath appointed me another seed instead of Abel, whom Cain slew" (Ge. 4:25). Eve knew that Seth, whose name means "substituted," (*Strong's Hebrew Dictionary*) was God's gift to take the place of the dear son she had lost. Seth would be God's chosen seed to carry on the godly line of men in a fallen world.

When Seth's son, Enos, was born, the Bible says that "men began to call upon the name of the LORD" (Ge. 4:26). It seems that God worked in a special way through Seth to draw people to seek the LORD. In the genealogy of Jesus Christ, recorded in Luke 3:38, we find that Jesus Christ was born in the line of Adam's son, Seth. God blessed Adam and Eve with many other sons and daughters (Ge. 5:4). All the people of the earth before the great flood descended from these children of Adam and Eve.

Many years later, in the line of Seth, a man named Noah was born. The Bible says that Noah was a "just" man. In other words, he was a man of faith in the true God- a man who "found grace in the eyes of the Lord" because he believed God's word (Ge. 6:8). Noah loved God and walked with God through prayer and fellowship with Him as a part of his daily life (Ge. 6:9). However, in Noah's time, the world had become so wicked that the only people who followed the LORD were Noah and his family. The entire race of mankind had followed the way of Cain. They had turned away from worshipping and serving the God who created them. By the time of Noah, things got so bad, and men were so wicked that God said He would destroy the entire world with a flood. God told Noah to build a great boat, an ark, to save his family. God also used Noah to warn the wicked people of his generation that God's judgment was coming. The Bible tells us in 2 Peter 2:5 that Noah was "a preacher of righteousness." He warned the people about the flood of God's judgment (1Pe. 3:20). God was longsuffering and gave the people one hundred twenty years to repent while Noah was building the ark. Sadly, only Noah's family believed God's warning and entered into the ark of safety.

Noah had three sons- Shem, Ham, and Japheth. Noah's sons and their wives, along with Noah and his wife, were the only ones who survived the great flood that engulfed the entire world. Everyone else perished. Noah and his sons were descendants of Seth, the son God gave Adam and Eve in place of Abel.

The world was repopulated by the three sons of Noah, and all of the people and the nations of the world today can be traced back to Noah's sons- Shem, Ham, and Japheth (Ge. 10). Though mankind had grievously failed the LORD and brought the great judgment of the flood upon the world, God would not fail to keep His promise. God had promised to send a Savior, and Noah alone had stayed true to God in his generation. God saved Noah and his family, and chose a descendant of Noah's son, Shem, to play a great part in the fulfillment of His promise. This teaches us an important truth- our choices matter. It is not a light thing to choose to walk away from God, and such a choice always brings sad consequences. On the other hand, to choose to serve God and love Him even when it seems everyone else is turning away, will always be rewarded by God; and, in the end, it will result in His peace and blessing even in the worst of times.

The Bible gives the account of a descendant of Shem by the name of Abraham who was born several generations after the great flood (Ge. 11:10). Abraham was Shem's great, great, great, great, great, great, great grandson. God had a very special plan for Abraham and his wife, Sarah. They were originally named Abram and Sarai- and are first mentioned in Genesis 11.

The Call of Abram and the Promise of a Son: Genesis 11:27-12:1-8:

"Now these *are* the generations of Terah: Terah begat Abram, Nahor, and Haran; and Haran begat Lot. And Haran died before his father Terah in the land of his nativity, in Ur of the Chaldees. And Abram and Nahor took them wives: the name of Abram's wife *was* Sarai; and the name of Nahor's wife, Milcah, the daughter of Haran, the father of Milcah, and the father of Iscah. But Sarai was barren; she *had* no child. And Terah took Abram his son, and Lot the son of Haran his son's son, and Sarai his daughter in law, his son Abram's wife; and they went forth with them from Ur of the Chaldees, to go into the land of Canaan; and they came unto Haran, and dwelt there. And the days of Terah were two hundred and five years: and Terah died in Haran. Now the LORD had said unto Abram, Get thee out of thy country, and from thy kindred, and from thy father's house, unto a land that I will shew thee: And I will make of thee a great nation, and I will bless thee, and make thy name great; and thou shalt be a blessing: And I will bless them that bless thee, and curse him that curseth thee: and in thee shall all families of the earth be blessed. So Abram departed, as the LORD had spoken unto him; and Lot went with him: and Abram *was* seventy and five years old when he departed out of Haran. And Abram took Sarai his wife, and Lot his brother's son, and all their substance that they had gathered, and the souls that they had gotten in Haran; and they went forth to go into the land of Canaan; and into the land of Canaan they came. And Abram passed through the land unto the place of Sichem, unto the plain of Moreh. And the Canaanite *was* then in the land. And the LORD appeared unto Abram, and said, Unto thy seed will I give this land: and there builded he an altar unto the LORD, who appeared unto him. And he removed from thence east: and there he builded an altar unto the LORD, and called upon the name of the LORD."

We find out several important things about Isaac's parents, Abram and Sarai, in this passage:

Abram and Sarai were from a city called Ur of the Chaldees. Ur was a prominent city in ancient Mesopotamia on the shore of the Euphrates River, south of Babylon. It was a very great city in Abram's day- great in population and great in cultural advancement. It was also great in wickedness. Ur was a center of idolatrous worship (*Bible Times and Ancient Kingdoms*, Cloud). Joshua 24:2 tells us that Abram's own father, Terah, worshipped idols; but Abram, unlike his father, chose to believe in the true God.

God told Abram to leave his own country, and his kindred, and his father's house to go to a land that the LORD would show him. Abram obeyed God and left Ur of the Chaldees; but his father, Terah, also went with him. They ended up stopping and settling for a while in a place called Haran. There Terah died, and Abram finally left Haran to go to the place where God had commanded him- the land of Canaan.

Abram and Sarai were faithful to the LORD, but they still faced sorrow and problems. One of the most heartbreaking things they faced was that Abram's wife, Sarai, was barren- she could not conceive a child (Ge. 11:30). How Abram and Sarai longed for a baby of their own! But the years went by, and no child came. Children are a blessing from the LORD (Ps. 127:3), so it must have been hard to understand why this blessing had been kept from Abram and Sarai, especially when they had left all and followed God to the place He had told them to go. Oftentimes, we don't understand difficult circumstances that come into our lives, especially when we are trying to obey God and do what is right. But God has a purpose for His children in suffering. Through suffering, God molds His children into people of humility and faith (Jas. 1:3-4). Abram and Sarai would see God move in a miraculous way to give them their heart's desire. But many years would pass until God's time came.

Perhaps you find yourself in a place like Abram and Sarai. You desire to see God work in your life and answer some specific need. God hears and answers prayer according to His will and time. Wait upon the Lord. Seek His face and His wisdom. His answers and timing are always perfect:

Ps 40:1-3 "I waited patiently for the LORD; and he inclined unto me, and heard my cry. He brought me up also out of an horrible pit, out of the miry clay, and set my feet upon a rock, *and* established my goings. And he hath put a new song in my mouth, *even* praise unto our God: many shall see *it*, and fear, and shall trust in the LORD."

"Content to Wait Upon God"

Content to wait upon God;
Content His face to seek;
Content to see His work;
His wondrous purpose meet.
Guided by His Spirit, His Word, His will, His way;
He will lead us safely as we follow day by day.
Content to wait upon God- Why should I anxious be?
My Savior goes before me; He will lead me tenderly.

-Evangeline Davis Bibb

Abram and Sarai would have to trust the LORD and His timing. They faced many challenges upon arriving in Canaan. In Abram's day, the land of Canaan was inhabited by various nations called Canaanites. The Canaanites were very wicked, idolatrous people.

The LORD appeared to Abram and promised him that He would give the land of Canaan to Abram's seed- his descendants -even though, at that time, Abram and Sarai still had no child. Abram built an altar and worshipped the LORD in the place where God appeared to him (Ge. 12:6-7).

Years later, Abram and Sarai remained childless. Abram wondered how God would fulfill His promise to make of him a great nation when he and Sarai were getting old and still had no child. God spoke to Abram again:

Ge 15:1-6 "After these things the word of the LORD came unto Abram in a vision, saying, Fear not, Abram: I *am* thy shield, *and* thy exceeding great reward. And Abram said, Lord GOD, what wilt thou give me, seeing I go childless, and the steward of my house *is* this Eliezer of Damascus? And Abram said, Behold, to me thou hast given no seed: and, lo, one born in my house is mine heir. And, behold, the word of the LORD *came* unto him, saying, This shall not be thine heir; but he that shall come forth out of thine own bowels shall be thine heir. And he brought him forth abroad, and said, Look now toward heaven, and tell the stars, if thou be able to number them: and he said unto him, So shall thy seed be. And he believed in the LORD; and he counted it to him for righteousness."

God promised Abram that he would have his own child. The descendants of that child would inherit the land of Canaan and become a great nation. Abram's descendants would be as numerous as the stars of heaven.

Genesis 15:6 tells us something very special- Abram "believed in the LORD and he counted it to him for righteousness." Abram was saved by faith. He believed God's promise was true. He knew he could trust what God said. If God promised to do something, He would do it. Abram didn't understand how it would all happen, but he knew he could trust God. We too are saved by believing that what God tells us is true. If we believe, as God says in His Word, that Jesus died for our sins and rose again from the dead, then God counts us righteous, just as He did Abram. We become God's own children because we believe in Him and trust Him for our salvation.

Abram and Sarai still had a lot to learn about trusting God. Sarai became impatient about not having a child. She was getting old. She thought perhaps God would give her and Abram a child some other way, so she decided to give her handmaid, an Egyptian woman named Hagar, to Abram to be his wife in hopes that Abram could have a son with her. Abram did have a son with Hagar. He named the child Ishmael. Sarai's idea was not God's plan, and it caused many problems for everyone concerned. Often, we too become impatient waiting for God to answer some prayer or to work His will in some important area of our lives. Time is passing away, and yet, God seems not to hear or to act. We become desperate for a solution and try to figure things out on our own. This can lead to disaster. God wants us to have His best. His timing is perfect if we will but wait for Him. Even when it seems all is lost, God can step in. Nothing is too hard for Him. Sadly, Abram and Sarai got ahead of God. The consequences caused heartache and sorrow, not only for Abram and Sarai, but for all the generations to follow. Yet, God is so merciful. He would still fulfill His promise to Abram and Sarai. God also promised to bless Abram's son, Ishmael. He too would become a mighty nation. Abram was eighty-six years old when Ishmael was born (Ge. 16).

The Birth of Isaac: Genesis 17:

Thirteen years later, when Abram was ninety-nine years old, the LORD appeared to him again:

Ge 17:1-8 "And when Abram was ninety years old and nine, the LORD appeared to Abram, and said unto him, I *am* the Almighty God; walk before me, and be thou perfect. And I will make my covenant between me and thee, and will multiply thee exceedingly. And Abram fell on his face: and God talked with him, saying, As for me, behold, my covenant *is* with thee, and thou shalt be a father of many nations. Neither shall thy name any more be called Abram, but thy name shall be Abraham; for a father of many nations have I made thee. And I will make thee exceeding fruitful, and I will make nations of thee, and kings shall come out of thee. And I will establish my covenant between me and thee and thy seed after thee in their generations for an everlasting covenant, to be a God unto thee, and to thy seed after thee. And I will give unto thee, and to thy seed after thee, the land wherein thou art a stranger, all the land of Canaan, for an everlasting possession; and I will be their God."

God told Abram that He would make him the father of many nations. God changed Abram's name to Abraham, a name that means "father of a multitude" (*Strong's Hebrew Dictionary*). God promised that He would give a special seed to Abraham and to his wife, Sarai. The nation descended from this child would be the heir of God's special blessings. God would give this nation the entire land of Canaan and would make an everlasting covenant (a sacred promise) with them. God Himself would be their God (Ge. 17:1-8). This nation would later be called "Israel."

God also changed Sarai's name to Sarah, which means "queen" (*Way of Life Encyclopedia*, Cloud). God said He would bless Sarah and give her a son. Sarah's son would be the one through whom God would fulfill His promise to send the Savior:

Ge 17:15-22 "And God said unto Abraham, As for Sarai thy wife, thou shalt not call her name Sarai, but Sarah *shall* her name *be*. And I will bless her, and give thee a son also of her: yea, I will bless her, and she shall be *a mother* of nations; kings of people shall be of her. Then Abraham fell upon his face, and laughed, and said in his heart, Shall *a child* be born unto him that is an hundred years old? and shall Sarah, that is ninety years old, bear? And Abraham said unto God, O that Ishmael might live before thee! And God said, Sarah thy wife shall bear thee a son indeed; and thou shalt call his name Isaac: and I will establish my covenant with him for an everlasting covenant, *and* with his seed after him. And as for Ishmael, I have heard thee: Behold, I have blessed him, and will make him fruitful, and will multiply him exceedingly; twelve princes shall he beget, and I will make him a great nation. But my covenant will I establish with Isaac, which Sarah shall bear unto thee at this set time in the next year. And he left off talking with him, and God went up from Abraham."

When Abraham heard God say that He would give Sarah a child, the Bible says that "Abraham fell upon his face and laughed!" Abraham was ninety-nine years old! He would be one hundred at the time God said they would have a son. Sarah was ninety years old! How could it be? But God said it would be so, and that the child's name was to be Isaac. The name Isaac means "laughter." The child's very name would remind Abraham that nothing is too hard for the LORD. God keeps His promises and does what is impossible! The LORD told Abraham that Sarah would have a son the very next year. God appeared to Abraham again in the plains of Mamre as Abraham sat in his tent door in the heat of the day. God reaffirmed His promise that He would give Sarah a son. Sarah was inside the tent when the LORD spoke to Abraham that day. When she heard what the LORD said, she laughed just as Abraham had when he heard the news. It seemed too hard to believe. She was so old. But God said in Genesis 18:14:

Ge 18:14 "Is any thing too hard for the LORD? At the time appointed I will return unto thee, according to the time of life, and Sarah shall have a son."

Sure enough, the following year, Isaac was born. His birth truly was a miracle! Oh how they laughed for joy then! God had given them a son just as He had promised. The account of Isaac's birth is found in Genesis 21:

Ge 21:1-7 "And the LORD visited Sarah as he had said, and the LORD did unto Sarah as he had spoken. For Sarah conceived, and bare Abraham a son in his old age, at the set time of which God had spoken to him. And Abraham called the name of his son that was born unto him, whom Sarah bare to him, Isaac. And Abraham circumcised his son Isaac being eight days old, as God had commanded him. And Abraham was an hundred years old, when his son Isaac was born unto him. And Sarah said, God hath made me to laugh, so that all that hear will laugh with me. And she said, Who would have said unto Abraham, that Sarah should have given children suck? for I have born him a son in his old age."

Isaac's parents found out that nothing is too hard for the LORD. How grateful they were for God's mercy, and how thankful they were that they had chosen to believe God. Hebrews 11 tells us about the faith of Isaac's parents, Abraham and Sarah:

Heb 11:8-12 "By faith Abraham, when he was called to go out into a place which he should after receive for an inheritance, obeyed; and he went out, not knowing whither he went. By faith he sojourned in the land of promise, as in a strange country, dwelling in tabernacles with Isaac and Jacob, the heirs with him of the same promise: For he looked for a city which hath foundations, whose builder and maker is God. Through faith also Sara herself received strength to conceive seed, and was delivered of a child when she was past age, because she judged him faithful who had promised. Therefore sprang there even of one, and him as good as dead, so many as the stars of the sky in multitude, and as the sand which is by the sea shore innumerable."

Abraham believed God, left Ur of the Chaldees, and went to the land of Canaan. He lived in tents in a strange country because he knew God would keep His word to him. He looked forward to the heavenly city, built by God Himself, as his eternal destination. Abraham's eternal home was so much more important than any earthly dwelling. Sarah also trusted God. She gave birth to the promised child when she was over ninety years old. From Abraham- a man so old that he was as good as dead when it came to having children –came a multitude of spiritual and physical descendants. The Savior, Jesus Christ, was born from the line of Abraham's promised son Isaac. Abraham is the father of all those who believe God's truth and accept His salvation through Christ. He is also the father of the nation of Israel through Sarah's only son, Isaac.

Be An Example

Abraham was also the father of many Gentile nations through his son, Ishmael, as well as other nations that descended from sons born to him after Sarah died. After Sarah died (Ge. 23:1-2), Abraham married a woman named Keturah, and God gave him sons through her (Ge. 25:1-4). Abraham believed God and was blessed with an innumerable multitude of both spiritual and physical descendants.

Personal Reflection:

What about you? Have you chosen to believe God's truth about His salvation through His only Son, Jesus Christ? If so, are you living like Abraham- are you looking for that heavenly city whose builder and maker is God? That should be our motivation every day- to live to please our Heavenly King. The Bible says it this way:

1Co 6:19-20 "What? know ye not that your body is the temple of the Holy Ghost *which is* in you, which ye have of God, and ye are not your own? For ye are bought with a price: therefore glorify God in your body, and in your spirit, which are God's."

1Co 10:31 "Whether therefore ye eat, or drink, or whatsoever ye do, do all to the glory of God."

Isaac's birth was miraculous. Like his father Abraham, Isaac would have to choose to trust God by faith even in times of trouble.

"Jesus, I My Cross Have Taken"

Jesus, I my cross have taken, all to leave and follow Thee;
Destitute, despised, forsaken, Thou from hence my all shall be.
Perish every fond ambition, all I've sought or hoped or known;
Yet how rich is my condition! God and heav'n are still mine own.

Let the world despise and leave me, they have left my Savior, too;
Human hearts and looks deceive me; Thou art not, like man, untrue.
And while Thou shalt smile upon me, God of wisdom, love and might,
Foes may hate and friends may shun me, show Thy face and all is bright.

Go, then, earthly fame and treasure! Come, disaster, scorn and pain!
In Thy service pain is pleasure; with Thy favor, loss is gain.

I have called Thee, "Abba, Father"; I have set my heart on Thee:
Storms may howl, and clouds may gather, all must work for good to me.

Man may trouble and distress me, 'twill but drive me to Thy breast;
Life with trials hard may press me; heav'n will bring me sweeter rest.
Oh, 'tis not in grief to harm me, while Thy love is left to me;
Oh, 'twere not in joy to charm me, were that joy unmixed with Thee.

Take, my soul, thy full salvation; rise o'er sin, and fear, and care;
Joy to find in every station something still to do or bear:
Think what Spirit dwells within thee; what a Father's smile is thine;
What a Savior died to win thee, child of heav'n, shouldst thou repine?

Haste then on from grace to glory, armed by faith, and winged by prayer,
Heav'n's eternal day's before thee, God's own hand shall guide thee there.
Soon shall close thy earthly mission, swift shall pass thy pilgrim days;
Hope shall change to glad fruition, faith to sight, and prayer to praise.

-Henry F. Lyte, 1833

Chapter 5: "The Life of Isaac" (Part 2)

Memory Verses:

Heb 11:1 "Now faith is the substance of things hoped for, the evidence of things not seen."

Heb 11:17-19 "By faith Abraham, when he was tried, offered up Isaac: and he that had received the promises offered up his only begotten *son*, Of whom it was said, That in Isaac shall thy seed be called: Accounting that God *was* able to raise *him* up, even from the dead; from whence also he received him in a figure."

Pr 3:5-6 "Trust in the LORD with all thine heart; and lean not unto thine own understanding. In all thy ways acknowledge him, and he shall direct thy paths."

Scripture Reading: Genesis 21-22

Key Lessons: Salvation, Obedience, and Faith

Abraham and Sarah experienced joy and laughter when God gave them their little son, Isaac. Abraham was one hundred years old, and Sarah was over ninety when Isaac was born. Abraham had another son named Ishmael by Sarah's handmaid, Hagar, the Egyptian. Ishmael was fourteen years old when Isaac was born (Ge. 16:16). But in Genesis 21, we see that more problems began to arise because of Hagar and Ishmael, which would have a lasting impact upon Isaac's life:

The Beginning of Persecution for the Promised Seed:

Ge 21:5-16 "And Abraham was an hundred years old, when his son Isaac was born unto him. And Sarah said, God hath made me to laugh, *so that* all that hear will laugh with me. And she said, Who would have said unto Abraham, that Sarah should have given children suck? for I have born *him* a son in his old age. And the child grew, and was weaned: and Abraham made a great feast the *same* day that Isaac was weaned. And Sarah saw the son of Hagar the Egyptian, which she had born unto Abraham, mocking. Wherefore she said unto Abraham, Cast out this bondwoman and her son: for the son of this bondwoman shall not be heir with my son, *even* with Isaac. And the thing was very grievous in Abraham's sight because of his son. And God said unto Abraham, Let it not be grievous in thy sight because of the lad, and because of thy bondwoman; in all that Sarah hath said unto thee, hearken unto her voice; **for in Isaac shall thy seed be called**. And also of the son of the bondwoman will I make a nation, because he *is* thy seed. And Abraham rose up early in the morning, and took bread, and a bottle of water, and gave *it* unto Hagar, putting *it* on her shoulder, and the child, and sent her away: and she departed, and wandered in the wilderness of Beersheba. And the water was spent in the bottle, and she cast the child under one of the shrubs. And she went, and sat her down over against *him* a good way off, as it were a bowshot: for she said, Let me not see the death of the child. And she sat over against *him*, and lift up her voice, and wept."

Abraham had prepared a great feast to celebrate a special milestone in his son Isaac's life. Isaac had been weaned and was old enough to eat regular food rather than be nursed by his mother. Weaning was a time of celebration and accomplishment in a boy's life- the first step toward becoming a man. In those days, mothers nursed their babies longer than mothers in the West do today. Isaac may have been anywhere from two to five years of age, perhaps even older. Whatever his age, he was very young. Ishmael was a young man, probably in his late teens, since he would have been around 14 when Isaac was born (Ge. 16:16-17:1, 21). Sarah saw Ishmael mocking and mistreating little Isaac. This threw her into a rage. You can imagine how she would feel to see a big boy like that picking on her little son- and on his special day. She went to Abraham and demanded that he cast out Hagar and her son Ishmael.

Abraham was grieved. He couldn't blame Sarah for being upset, but Ishmael was his son too. He loved him. What should he do? It was then that God spoke to Abraham again. God told Abraham to listen to Sarah. She was right in this case. God said, "In Isaac shall thy seed be called." Isaac was to be the heir to God's special blessing and promise. It was through Isaac that God would raise up His people, Israel; and it was through Isaac's seed that God would send the promised Savior. As painful as it was, the time had come for a separation. Hagar and Ishmael needed to go; but God told Abraham that He would bless Ishmael and make a nation of him also because he was Abraham's seed. Early the next morning, Abraham rose up, gave Hagar some bread and water, and sent her and Ishmael away. It must have been hard for Abraham to say goodbye to his son, but he knew he could trust God to keep His promise. God would take care of Ishmael. After Hagar and Ishmael left, things became very difficult for them. They wandered in the desert of Beersheba until their water was gone. Before long, they were dying of thirst. Hagar left her son Ishmael under a shrub. She sat down a good way off with her back to him and began to weep aloud. She couldn't bear to watch her son die. He was suffering so. But God did not forget Hagar and Ishmael or His promise to Abraham. It was then that God spoke to Hagar:

Ge 21:17-21: "And God heard the voice of the lad; and the angel of God called to Hagar out of heaven, and said unto her, What aileth thee, Hagar? fear not; for God hath heard the voice of the lad where he *is*. Arise, lift up the lad, and hold him in thine hand; for I will make him a great nation. And God opened her eyes, and she saw a well of water; and she went, and filled the bottle with water, and gave the lad drink. And God was with the lad; and he grew, and dwelt in the wilderness, and became an archer. And he dwelt in the wilderness of Paran: and his mother took him a wife out of the land of Egypt."

God saved Hagar and Ishmael and blessed the boy as He had promised. Ishmael grew strong and had twelve sons who became princes of their own nations (Ge. 25:16). The separation of Abraham from his son, Ishmael, was hard but it was for the best for both Ishmael and Isaac. God had a special plan for Isaac and that plan meant that he must be the heir of all the promises that God had given to Abraham.

Abraham's Greatest Test of Faith:

Years passed. God continued to bless Abraham, and Isaac grew to be a strong, young man. It was at that time that Abraham faced the greatest test of his life. Would he trust God with his most precious treasure- his son, Isaac? Would Isaac trust and obey his father, Abraham? We find the answer in Genesis 22:

Ge. 22:1-3 "And it came to pass after these things, that God did tempt Abraham, and said unto him, Abraham: and he said, Behold, *here* I *am*. And he said, Take now thy son, thine only *son* Isaac, whom thou lovest, and get thee into the land of Moriah; and offer him there for a burnt offering upon one of the mountains which I will tell thee of. And Abraham rose up early in the morning, and saddled his ass, and took two of his young men with him, and Isaac his son, and clave the wood for the burnt offering, and rose up, and went unto the place of which God had told him."

The word "tempt" in verse one means "to try" or "to prove." God does not tempt anyone to do evil (Jas. 1:13). God was testing the faith of Abraham. As God's very dear and special servant, Abraham's faith was very precious to the Lord. Through this test, God would show Abraham His great love for him, and Abraham's obedience would show his faith and love for God. Abraham had trusted God with everything- his home, his family, his possessions, his wife, and his son, Ishmael- now, God asked Abraham to trust Him with the most precious person in his life- his beloved son, Isaac.

God called Abraham by his name- that name that He had given Abram that meant "father of a multitude" (*Strongs Hebrew Dictionary*). Even in this test, God's promise to Abraham would not fail. Abraham's immediate response to God was, "Behold, here I am." Abraham was willing to do whatever God wanted. The Lord knew how much Isaac meant to Abraham. How he loved him! He was his beloved son. When God spoke to Abraham of Isaac, He called him, "thine only son." The word translated "only" is the Hebrew word "yachiyd *yaw-kheed*" which means "beloved" or "precious." It also means "only" in the sense of solitary or "by himself" (*Strongs*). Isaac was the sole heir to all that Abraham possessed and the son who would inherit God's promised blessing. Isaac was Abraham's only son through his wife Sarah and the son through whom the prophesied Savior would come.

God told Abraham to take his precious son and offer him as a burnt offering upon one of the mountains he would tell him of. This command of God sounds very shocking to us, but to Abraham sacrifice- blood sacrifice -was a part of worship to the LORD. Yet, it was an innocent and perfect animal that God required in worship as a picture of the innocent and perfect Savior to come. God's command to Abraham was a test of his love and obedience. Abraham knew that after all God had done, he could trust Him to keep His word to him.

<u>The Obedience of Abraham:</u>

Abraham did not question God. He did not argue with God. He did not hesitate. He trusted God to keep His promises concerning Isaac. The Bible says that "Abraham rose up early in the morning, and saddled his ass, and took two of his young men with him, and Isaac his son, and clave the wood for the burnt offering, and rose up, and went unto the place of which God had told him." This certainly did not mean that Abraham did not grieve in his heart for what he must do to his dear son, but God gave Abraham grace to obey. Abraham loved Isaac, but he loved God more. This was the test of that love. God had been good to Abraham and ever faithful. Abraham was grateful. He would be faithful to the Lord, no matter what the cost:

Ge 22:4-5 "Then on the third day Abraham lifted up his eyes, and saw the place afar off. And Abraham said unto his young men, Abide ye here with the ass; and I and the lad will go yonder and worship, and come again to you."

The Picture Shown by Abraham's Faith:

For two days Abraham, his servants, and Isaac travelled to the place God told Abraham to go. On the third day, Abraham saw the place afar off. Abraham's words to the young men travelling with them show us his true heart. Abraham trusted God. He said, "I and the lad will go yonder and worship, and **come again unto you.**" Abraham knew what God had promised him. God had promised to make of Isaac's seed a great nation. Isaac was an unmarried young man at this time and had no son. God had not yet fulfilled His promise through Isaac, and Abraham knew God's promise would never fail. He knew that somehow, both he and Isaac would return together from worshipping the Lord. In fact, Hebrews 11:17-19 tells us exactly what was in Abraham's mind at that time:

Heb 11:17-19 "By faith Abraham, when he was tried, offered up Isaac: and he that had received the promises offered up his only begotten *son*, Of whom it was said, That in Isaac shall thy seed be called: Accounting that God *was* able to raise *him* up, even from the dead..."

Abraham knew that even after he offered Isaac up as a burnt offering to the Lord, God was able to raise Isaac up from the dead. What faith in God Abraham had! The last part of Hebrews 11:19 says, "Accounting that God was able to raise him up even from the dead **from whence also he received him in a figure.**" God gives us a very important truth through the words Abraham spoke to his servants. By believing that God could raise Isaac up from the dead, Abraham's faith was pointing to something- and Someone -far more important than himself and his son, Isaac. Abraham's faith was pointing to another Father- God the Father -who would give up His Son, Jesus Christ, to be sacrificed and raised from the dead. Abraham is a picture of God the Father giving His only Son for sinners like you and me. Isaac is a picture of Christ, the only begotten Son of God, being offered for the sins of the world. This is the "figure"- the picture -that God was showing through Abraham's obedience. By faith, Abraham portrayed that picture and received the truth concerning the Christ to come. We will see more of this wondrous picture as we finish the story.

The Unwavering Faith of Abraham:

Ge 22:6-8 "And Abraham took the wood of the burnt offering, and laid *it* upon Isaac his son; and he took the fire in his hand, and a knife; and they went both of them together. And Isaac spake unto Abraham his father, and said, My father: and he said, Here *am* I, my son. And he said, Behold the fire and the wood: but where *is* the lamb for a burnt offering? And Abraham said, My son, God will provide himself a lamb for a burnt offering: so they went both of them together."

Abraham would not shrink from obeying the command of the Lord. He obeyed all the way to the end. He saw the place in the distance and prepared to offer his only son to the Lord. God had a wondrous purpose and plan in all that He asked Abraham to do. Abraham loved God. There was no turning back now. He had trusted God this far. He would go all the way. The Bible says that Abraham took the wood needed for the burnt offering "and laid it upon Isaac his son." Do you see the picture that God gave us in this? One day, God Himself would allow a cross of wood to be laid upon the back of His only Son, the Lord Jesus Christ, to carry toward another hill -Mount Calvary. The Lord Jesus willingly bore that cross of wood for us, that He might suffer, and die, and pay the penalty for our sin. The wood laid upon Isaac's back was a picture of what Jesus would do for us in that day to come.

Abraham then took the fire in his hand- some hot coals or a torch -to light the fire that would be used to consume his own son as a burnt offering. The fire is also a picture for us. In the Bible, fire is symbolic of God's judgment upon sin. God is just and holy. He cannot allow sin to go unpunished. When Christ died upon the cross, He bore all the fire of God's judgment that our sins deserve to save us from the eternal fire of hell. All the wrath of God that sinners deserve was poured out upon His own Son, Jesus Christ -the innocent Lamb of God.

Finally, Abraham took a knife, the instrument he would use to slay his own son. One day, God would allow wicked, sinful men to nail His own Son to the cross to die for sinners. So we see that in all these things that Abraham did, God was giving us a picture of the sacrifice He would make for all mankind. When Abraham laid the wood upon his son's back, Isaac asked an important question. He saw all the things needed for the sacrifice- the fire and the wood -but where was the lamb? Isaac certainly had worshipped the LORD with his father on many occasions. He knew a blood sacrifice from a spotless lamb was required. Abraham's answer showed his continued faith and also proclaimed a prophecy concerning what God would do for us to provide our salvation: "My son, God will provide himself a lamb for a burnt offering." Indeed, God would provide Himself. The Son of God, Himself, would be the Lamb slain to take away our sin.

The Obedience and Submission of Isaac:

Isaac was satisfied with his father's answer. After Abraham's answer, we do not read that Isaac resisted or questioned his father in any way. He simply trusted and obeyed. They went on together to the place of sacrifice.

Ge 22:9-10 "And they came to the place which God had told him of; and Abraham built an altar there, and laid the wood in order, and bound Isaac his son, and laid him on the altar upon the wood. And Abraham stretched forth his hand, and took the knife to slay his son."

Through all of this, Isaac did not resist his father, but submitted himself as a willing sacrifice. Even as his father bound him and raised the knife to slay him, he quietly waited, trusting his father. This too is a picture of the Lord Jesus. Isaiah 53 tells us of the sufferings that Jesus would go through willingly for us:
Isa 53:7 "He was oppressed, and he was afflicted, yet he opened not his mouth: he is brought as a lamb to the slaughter, and as a sheep before her shearers is dumb, so he openeth not his mouth."

Christ had the power to free Himself from those who would crucify Him, yet He willingly submitted to suffer and die for us. He did not resist or protest, but silently endured all of His suffering that He might provide our salvation. Isaac was a picture of our submissive Savior as he willingly and silently endured being bound and laid upon the altar in obedience to his father.

Abraham's Faith Rewarded- God's Substitute Given:

Abraham was willing to do all that God said. He raised the knife, ready to plunge it into his son. Then, he heard a wonderful sound:

Ge 22:11-14 "And the angel of the LORD called unto him out of heaven, and said, Abraham, Abraham: and he said, Here *am* I. And he said, Lay not thine hand upon the lad, neither do thou any thing unto him: for now I know that thou fearest God, seeing thou hast not withheld thy son, thine only *son* from me. And Abraham lifted up his eyes, and looked, and behold behind *him* a ram caught in a thicket by his horns: and Abraham went and took the ram, and offered him up for a burnt offering in the stead of his son. And Abraham called the name of that place Jehovah-jireh: as it is said *to* this day, In the mount of the LORD it shall be seen."

Oh, what joy Abraham must have felt! He would not have to sacrifice his son. He had passed the test. God knew how much Abraham loved and trusted Him. God provided a substitute for the life of Abraham's son, Isaac. How Abraham and Isaac must have rejoiced together and embraced one another as Abraham unbound his son and took him off of that altar and offered the ram in his place. In this we see again the wondrous plan of God for our salvation. "The wages of sin is death..." All of us deserve death- eternal death in hell. "But the gift of God is eternal life..."- through our substitute -"Jesus Christ our Lord" (Ro. 6:23). Hallelujah, for our Savior!

Isaac is a picture of us all. He was a sinner condemned to die, but God provided the ram to die in his place. God provided Jesus Christ, the Lamb of God, to be our substitute. He died in our place so that we would not have to suffer the eternal death of hell. He took our death upon the cross so that we could go free and receive His salvation. But to receive His salvation, we must be willing to accept Christ as our substitute and Savior. What if Isaac had refused the ram God had provided as his substitute? What if in pride he had exclaimed, "No, wait a minute! I am going to be the hero of this story. I can die for myself!" That would have been a foolish end, wouldn't it? But that is the foolish end of every person who refuses Christ as Savior and trusts his own way. Thankfully, Isaac humbly accepted the substitute God provided. You can too. You can go free to day and look forward to an eternal home in Heaven if you will trust the Savior God provided- Jesus Christ.

<u>The Special Name of the Mount</u>:

Abraham called the place where God showed His salvation "Jehovah-jireh" which means, "Jehovah will see" (*Strong's Hebrew Dictionary*). In this place God showed a picture of His salvation through Christ. Thousands of years later, in this same place, Jesus Christ, the Messiah, would suffer, shed His blood, and die in the place of sinners on a cruel cross. Isaiah prophesied about the suffering of the Messiah and how Jehovah would see Christ's sacrifice and suffering for sinners and be satisfied. The sinner's debt would be fully paid by the sinless Savior:

Isa 53:5-11 "But he *was* wounded for our transgressions, *he was* bruised for our iniquities: the chastisement of our peace *was* upon him; and with his stripes we are healed. All we like sheep have gone astray; we have turned every one to his own way; and the LORD hath laid on him the iniquity of us all. He was oppressed, and he was afflicted, yet he opened not his mouth: he is brought as a lamb to the slaughter, and as a sheep before her shearers is dumb, so he openeth not his mouth. He was taken from prison and from judgment: and who shall declare his generation? for he was cut off out of the land of the living: for the transgression of my people was he stricken. And he made his grave with the wicked, and with the rich in his death; because he had done no violence, neither *was any* deceit in his mouth. Yet it pleased the LORD to bruise him; he hath put *him* to grief: when thou shalt make his soul an offering for sin, he shall see *his* seed, he shall prolong *his* days, and the pleasure of the LORD shall prosper in his hand. <u>He shall see of the travail of his soul, *and* shall be satisfied</u>: by his knowledge shall my righteous servant justify many; for he shall bear their iniquities."

This name "Jehovah-Jireh" points to the coming of the Savior to the very place where God provided a substitute for Isaac, Abraham's precious son. Over eight hundred years after the time of Abraham, the temple of the LORD was built by Solomon upon Mount Moriah (2Ch. 3:1). Moriah was the place where Abraham prepared to offer Isaac, his son, as a sacrifice to the LORD. Solomon's temple was later destroyed by the Babylonians because of Israel's disobedience and idolatry; but when God brought a remnant of His people back to the land of Israel, the temple was rebuilt upon Mount Moriah. The return of the Jews from the Babylonian exile and the rebuilding of the temple are detailed in the book of Ezra. The temple in Jerusalem that was standing in Jesus' day was that same rebuilt temple, greatly expanded by King Herod. Christ, Himself, the Lamb of God, stood in that temple- God in the flesh -the Savior who came to offer Himself for the sins of the world. God's salvation was plainly seen when Christ shed His blood upon Calvary, just outside the city of Jerusalem. This was the wondrous picture God showed through Abraham and Isaac's obedience! In the mount of the LORD, Christ was seen!

I'm so thankful that both Abraham and his son, Isaac, trusted and obeyed God. I'm especially thankful that God provided a Savior, the precious Lamb of God, to die in our place.

Be An Example

<u>Personal Reflection</u>

Have you trusted God for your salvation by taking Jesus as your substitute? If not, you can do so today. God longs to save you. The Bible says in Romans 10:13 "For whosoever shall call upon the name of the Lord shall be saved." Salvation is a free gift that God has provided. We need only to come to Him in faith to receive it:

Joh 3:16 "For God so loved the world, that he gave his only begotten Son, that whosoever believeth in him should not perish, but have everlasting life."

Ro 10:9 "That if thou shalt confess with thy mouth the Lord Jesus, and shalt believe in thine heart that God hath raised him from the dead, thou shalt be saved."

If you have trusted Christ as your Savior, He is your blessed Redeemer and Friend. Walk with Him today. Thank Him for the wondrous salvation He provided, and share that precious gift with others.

"Blessed Redeemer"

Up Calv'ry's mountain, one dreadful morn,
Walked Christ my Savior, weary and worn;
Facing for sinners death on the cross,
That He might save them from endless loss.

Refrain:
Blessed Redeemer! Precious Redeemer!
Seems now I see Him on Calvary's tree;
Wounded and bleeding, for sinners pleading,
Blind and unheeding—dying for me!

"Father forgive them!" thus did He pray,
E'en while His lifeblood flowed fast away;
Praying for sinners while in such woe—
No one but Jesus ever loved so.

Oh, how I love Him, Savior and Friend,
How can my praises ever find end!

Through years unnumbered on heaven's shore,
My tongue shall praise Him forevermore.

-Avis M. Christiansen, 1920

Be An Example

Chapter 6: "The Life of Joseph" (Part 1)

Memory Verses:

Ps 40:1-3 "I waited patiently for the LORD; and he inclined unto me, and heard my cry. He brought me up also out of an horrible pit, out of the miry clay, and set my feet upon a rock, *and* established my goings. And he hath put a new song in my mouth, *even* praise unto our God: many shall see *it*, and fear, and shall trust in the LORD."

Ro 8:28 "And we know that all things work together for good to them that love God, to them who are the called according to *his* purpose."

Scripture Reading: Genesis 30:22-24; 37:1-4

Key Lessons: Faith and patience through trials and persecution; the dangers of envy and evil speaking

Have you ever suffered for doing what was right? Have you ever been falsely accused or cruelly misjudged? Being misjudged is one of the hardest things to endure when you're trying to do what is right. Sometimes we feel like giving up, but God has a purpose in our trials. He will give us the strength to endure if we trust Him. The Bible says:

Ga 6:9 "And let us not be weary in well doing: for in due season we shall reap, if we faint not."

God rewards those who stay true to Him and to His Word even in the face of trials. One of the greatest examples of someone in the Bible who persevered through trials was Joseph. Joseph went through some very hard times and great temptations, but through it all, we never read that he turned away from doing what was right and obeying God. God blessed Joseph because he chose to trust and obey no matter what came. We can learn so much from the life of this faithful young man.

Joseph's Family: Genesis 24-30:

Joseph was the grandson of Isaac, Abraham's son. God blessed Isaac, just as He had promised Abraham He would. Isaac had two twin sons, Esau and Jacob. Isaac's wife's name was Rebekah (Ge. 25). Though Jacob was the younger of the two boys, he was the son that God chose to become the father of the nation of Israel. In fact, later in Jacob's life, God changed his name to "Israel," a name that means "having power with God" (*Way of Life Encyclopedia*, Cloud). Jacob ended up marrying two wives- two sisters, in fact -named Rachel and Leah. Jacob loved Rachel, the younger sister, but Rachel's father tricked Jacob into marrying his older daughter Leah first. In order to have Rachel- the wife he loved -Jacob ended up marrying both of Laban's daughters (Ge. 29). Again, the idea of multiple wives was not God's plan for marriage. This situation caused a lot of problems for Jacob and his family. In fact, Jacob eventually ended up with four wives because Rachel and Leah followed Sarah's unwise pattern of giving their handmaids to Jacob to be his wives as well.

God was merciful to Jacob and his family in spite of all these things, but the family problems greatly affected his son Joseph's life. For one thing, Jacob did not love Leah. Because Leah was not loved, God had compassion on her and blessed her with children. Altogether, Leah had six sons- Reuben, Simeon, Levi, Judah, Issachar, and Zebulun. Leah also had a daughter named Dinah. It is interesting to note here, that it was through the line of Judah, a son of Leah, that the Savior, the Lord Jesus Christ, was born.

Rachel, the wife Jacob loved, was barren. She had no children. It plagued her heart to have no child as she watched her sister give birth to one child after another. Finally, in desperation, Rachel gave Jacob her handmaid, Bilhah, to be his wife so she could at least have sons through her handmaid. Rachel's handmaid had two sons- Dan and Naphtali. Not to be outdone, Leah gave Jacob her handmaid to be his wife so she could have even more sons through her. Leah's handmaid, Zilpah, also had two sons- Gad and Asher.

Finally, after many years, God blessed Rachel with her own son. His name was Joseph. When Joseph was born, Rachel knew that God had heard her prayer and would bless her with another son:

Ge 30:22-24 "And God remembered Rachel, and God hearkened to her, and opened her womb. And she conceived, and bare a son; and said, God hath taken away my reproach: And she called his name Joseph; and said, The LORD shall add to me another son."

Years later, when Joseph was still a teenager, his mother Rachel did give birth to another son, Benjamin. Rachel died when Benjamin was born, but God had heard and answered her prayers. God blessed Rachel with two sons, and one day, Joseph would be God's instrument to save her entire family. From the time he was born, Joseph was the most beloved son of his father, Jacob, because he was the son of his old age. The biblical account of Joseph's life starts when he was seventeen years of age:

Joseph, the Dear and Obedient Son of his Father: Genesis 37:1-4:

Ge 37: 1-3 "And Jacob dwelt in the land wherein his father was a stranger, in the land of Canaan. These *are* the generations of Jacob. Joseph, *being* seventeen years old, was feeding the flock with his brethren; and the lad *was* with the sons of Bilhah, and with the sons of Zilpah, his father's wives: and Joseph brought unto his father their evil report. Now Israel loved Joseph more than all his children, because he *was* the son of his old age: and he made him a coat of *many* colours."

In this passage, the Bible gives us more of the history of Jacob's family. The key character God focuses on is Jacob's young son, Joseph. Jacob, his wives, and his children still lived in the land of Canaan- the land that God had called Abraham to go to so many years before. Hebrews 11:9 tells us that Abraham, Isaac, and Jacob dwelt in "tabernacles" in "the land of promise." They lived in tents in the land that God had promised to give to Abraham's seed, the future nation of Israel. All these years, Abraham, Isaac, and Jacob had lived in Canaan as strangers in a foreign land. But God would keep His promise to them. One day, Canaan would belong to their family and to the great nation that would descend from them just as God had said. At the time of Joseph's youth, however, Jacob's family still lived as nomadic shepherds in Canaan.

Joseph's Courage and the Danger of Hidden Sin:

God had blessed Jacob with large flocks of sheep and goats when he lived with and worked for his father in law, Laban, years before. These flocks provided milk, meat, and wool that the family needed to live. Taking care of the flocks was a great responsibility. Jacob's son, Joseph, was out feeding the flocks with some of his half-brothers- the sons of Bilhah and Zilpah. Joseph's brothers were doing things they knew they shouldn't do while they were out with the flocks. We aren't told what they were doing, but it was clearly something they knew their father would not approve of. Joseph knew it too, and he could not be silent about it and remain obedient to his father.

Sometimes we think that because our parents or other authority figures are not around, we can get away with doing things that are wrong- especially when others are doing it. After all, no one is going to know about it, right? Wrong! God sees everything. Hidden sin does so much damage to our lives- and, sin will always come out -one way or another:

Ga 6:7-8 "Be not deceived; God is not mocked: for whatsoever a man soweth, that shall he also reap. For he that soweth to his flesh shall of the flesh reap corruption; but he that soweth to the Spirit shall of the Spirit reap life everlasting."

Pr 28:13, "He that covereth his sins shall not prosper: but whoso confesseth and forsaketh *them* shall have mercy."

Nu 32:23 "But if ye will not do so, behold, ye have sinned against the LORD: and be sure your sin will find you out."

Joseph's brothers thought they could live however they pleased when their father wasn't around, but God made sure their sin found them out. He used the faithful young Joseph to expose their wrongdoing. Joseph was a man of courage and obedience. He knew that what his brothers were doing out in the fields was wrong. He did not cover their sin. He knew the right thing to do was to be obedient to his father and to God, so "Joseph brought unto his father their evil report." Joseph was not being a snitch or a tattletale. He was being obedient. It's hard to stand up and tell the truth about something when everyone else is doing it, but Joseph was right to do so. In fact, true love for others is to do what is best for them, even when they may hate and persecute us for it.

Have you ever had to tell on someone for their own good because you knew what they were doing was wrong and would hurt them and others in the end? It's a hard thing to do, but it's always right to stand with godly authority. We should urge others to do right and give them an opportunity to correct their behavior, but ultimately, if they refuse good counsel, we must bring authority to bear upon them to save them and others from evil and harm. We must obey God rather than trying to please our peers. Standing for truth is honoring God. The Bible says we are to obey God rather than men, and that's exactly what Joseph did in telling on his brothers. Sadly, they did not repent of their wrong. Rather, they hated and despised Joseph for exposing them.

The Blessings of Obedience:

Because of his obedience, Joseph received the love and approval of his father and special blessings from him. The Bible says that Israel, God's name for Jacob, "loved Joseph more than all his children, because he was the son of his old age: and he made him a coat of many colours." Joseph was a special blessing to Jacob. He was the son of his old age- and he was an obedient son. Jacob loved Joseph very dearly. The coat that Jacob gave to Joseph was a picture of the love that Jacob had for his son. Clothing was a very precious commodity. It wasn't easy to come by in those days. You couldn't just jump on a camel and ride over to the local clothing store to buy a new coat. Cloth had to be handwoven, and clothing was made through a long, laborious process of spinning the thread, dying it, and weaving it into cloth. A well-made coat gave warmth and protection from wind, cold, and weather. Since Jacob's family lived in tents in the desert, the protection of clothing was vital to their survival. To have a coat of many colors would take many days and hours of work to spin the thread, dye the various thread colors, and then weave it into a fine garment. The coat Jacob gave Joseph was very special. For Joseph, it was a precious gift that pictured the love of his dear father. Every time Joseph put that coat on, he was reminded of his father's love for him.

For the Christian, Joseph's coat pictures the special love that God pours out upon His obedient children. When we choose to love and obey God, we receive blessings of His presence and truth that others far from God do not know. Joseph's coat is a picture of the many graces and blessings that God pours out on those who love and walk with Him.

The Bitterness and Envy of Joseph's Brothers and the Danger of Evil Speaking:

Sadly, Joseph's brothers did not view Joseph or his coat with love. His coat only reminded them of the fact that their father loved Joseph best. Their disobedience to their father did not help them find favor in his sight. The more foolishly they behaved, the more their father distrusted them. Unfortunately, they did not learn from Joseph's obedience. Instead, they hated Joseph for telling the truth about them, and they hated the fact that he was blessed and loved by their father. Their attitude at this time reminds us a lot of another brother we read about- Cain. Cain hated his brother Abel because God approved of him (Ge. 4; 1 Jo. 3:12). Joseph's brothers hated him for the same reason. Every time Joseph gained his father's approval and love, his brothers grew more resentful. They did not change their own ways. They only hated Joseph more.

Ge 37:4 "And when his brethren saw that their father loved him more than all his brethren, they hated him, and could not speak peaceably unto him."

Joseph's brothers were bitter against him. Bitterness eats away at our hearts if we let it take root. It destroys love and brings hatred into our soul. Often when we are jealous of someone else, we begin to talk badly about them to others. As we will see, this is what happened among Joseph's brothers. When they saw him coming, the hatred rose up in their hearts, and they spoke evil of him among themselves. This kind of evil speaking only caused their hatred to grow. The Bible warns against speaking evil against others:

Jas 4:11 "Speak not evil one of another, brethren. He that speaketh evil of *his* brother, and judgeth his brother, speaketh evil of the law, and judgeth the law: but if thou judge the law, thou art not a doer of the law, but a judge."

To speak evil of someone is to falsely accuse them. The Greek word used in James 4 is "katalaleo" and it means to slander someone (*Strong's Greek Dictionary*). A slander is "a false tale or report maliciously uttered and tending to injure the reputation of another by lessening him in the esteem of his fellow citizens"

(*Webster's1828 Dictionary*). So, evil speaking is spreading lies about someone with the intent to hurt their reputation. Envy is often the thing that motivates evil speaking. Sometimes, we think we know the motive and heart of someone else, and we begin to accuse them to others ("She thinks she's so ____.") When we do this, we are judging the heart - something that only God can know -and we cease to obey God's law ourselves. It's one thing to see someone doing wrong and try to help them get right with the Lord. It's another thing to think we can judge someone's heart and motives and begin to tear them down to others. Love tries to help people who are in the wrong to get right. Love does not hate and tear others down:

Eph 4:29 "Let no corrupt communication proceed out of your mouth, but that which is good to the use of edifying, that it may minister grace unto the hearers."

Teasing and making fun of others is another way that envy and slander often come out. Christians are to encourage one another in the Lord and build each other up in God. We are to esteem each other as better than ourselves (Php. 2:3). Humor at the expense of others does not please God. Joseph's brothers used this tactic also, as we will see. If your words are being used to make fun of someone or to make them feel small, they are not godly words. Godly words give life and truth, and encourage others to follow the Lord.

Sadly, Joseph's brothers used their words to spread hatred and bitterness among themselves. They used their words to try to hurt Joseph. This is what the devil does among God's people too. He is the accuser of God's people (Re. 12:10). Satan loves nothing more than for Christians to accuse one another and to plant wicked thoughts in the minds of others concerning other brothers and sisters in Christ. He wants God's people to sow discord and hatred among themselves. This is not God's way for His people; in fact, the Bible tells us in Proverbs 6:19, that sowing discord among brethren is an "abomination" to God. It is something so wicked before God that it disgusts Him. It makes God sick. Evil speaking and sowing discord are part of the devil's plan to hurt and destroy God's work and His people. So much heartache comes from speaking evil of others. Joseph's brothers found this out the hard way.

Joseph's brothers brought misery upon themselves by their disobedience. It wasn't Joseph's fault, but they wanted to blame someone else for their sin. When Joseph told on them, they turned on him. If we are involved in sin, we often want to blame someone else. If you remember, that is what Adam and Eve did when they sinned against God. They were trying to hide their sin as well, but they couldn't hide from God. The same was true for Joseph's brothers. They didn't listen to God, and their sin blinded their eyes to the truth.

The Longsuffering Attitude of Joseph:

The grace of God was so evident in how Joseph responded to his brothers. Even though Joseph's brother's hated him, he did not hate them in return. In this as well as in many other things, Joseph was an example of the Lord Jesus Christ. He did not let bitterness fill his heart even though his brothers mistreated him. This is how God wants us to live as Christians. We are to love others as God loves us. There is no place for hatred of others in the heart of a Christian. We may hate the bad things that people do and say; and if we love God, we should certainly hate sin as He does. But Jesus said we are to love and pray for our enemies and for those who mistreat us. In doing this, we love as God loves, for He loved us while we were yet sinners and gave Himself for our salvation. Jesus said:

Mt 5:44-45 "But I say unto you, Love your enemies, bless them that curse you, do good to them that hate you, and pray for them which despitefully use you, and persecute you; That ye may be the children of your Father which is in heaven: for he maketh his sun to rise on the evil and on the good, and sendeth rain on the just and on the unjust."

The Bible also says:

1 Joh 2:11 "But he that hateth his brother is in darkness, and walketh in darkness, and knoweth not whither he goeth, because that darkness hath blinded his eyes."

If we have a bitter heart toward someone, even someone who has hurt us very deeply, the best cure is prayer. We can pray that God will take the bitterness away from us and show us the truth about His love for that person. Then we can truly begin to pray for them with God's love in our hearts. Remember, God loved us while we were yet sinners. Our sins nailed Jesus Christ to a cross. God provided forgiveness for us even before we knew to ask for it. That is amazing love, isn't it? And nothing is worth losing the blessings of our Heavenly Father because of bitterness. When we get things right with God, we can have joy and sweet fellowship with Him once again. And God can work in the hearts of those who have hurt us. The bitterness and hatred Joseph's brothers had led to so much heartache and sorrow for them, for Joseph, and for their father. How much better it would have been if they had repented of their disobedience and followed Joseph's example. But they did not, and their bitter hatred led to terrible acts. That is the course of sin if we let it go its way. If we do not deal with its start in our hearts, it will end in action that cannot be undone.

Personal Reflection:

What about you? Is there some hidden sin in your life? If you will admit it to God and turn away from it, the Bible says, He will have mercy and forgive you and give you strength to obey Him. Do you have bitterness in your heart toward someone? God can remove that bitterness if you will ask Him. He can replace your bitterness with His love. Begin to pray for the person who has hurt you. God can do things in the hearts of others that we never can. He can turn situations around that seem impossible to us. Is there envy in your heart toward someone else because they are loved and appreciated more than you? Perhaps the problem lies in your own disobedience. Perhaps God is waiting for you to change your behavior or to reach out to that person you are envious of and be a blessing to them. Pray that God will give you a right heart and strength to obey Him. Do you need courage to stand for what's right even when others around you are doing wrong? God can give you courage, like Joseph, to do right no matter what others are doing.

"Living For Jesus"

Living for Jesus, a life that is true,
Striving to please Him in all that I do;
Yielding allegiance, glad-hearted and free,
This is the pathway of blessing for me.

Refrain:
O Jesus, Lord and Savior, I give myself to Thee,
For Thou, in Thy atonement, didst give Thyself for me;
I own no other Master, my heart shall be Thy throne;
My life I give, henceforth to live, O Christ, for Thee alone.

Living for Jesus Who died in my place,
Bearing on Calv'ry my sin and disgrace;
Such love constrains me to answer His call,
Follow His leading and give Him my all.

Be An Example

Living for Jesus, wherever I am,
Doing each duty in His holy Name;
Willing to suffer affliction and loss,
Deeming each trial a part of my cross.

Living for Jesus through earth's little while,
My dearest treasure, the light of His smile;
Seeking the lost ones He died to redeem,
Bringing the weary to find rest in Him.

-Thomas O. Chisholm, 1917

Chapter 7: "The Life of Joseph" (Part 2)

Memory Verses:

Ro 8:28 "And we know that all things work together for good to them that love God, to them who are the called according to *his* purpose."

Ps 37:4-5 "Delight thyself also in the LORD; and he shall give thee the desires of thine heart. Commit thy way unto the LORD; trust also in him; and he shall bring *it* to pass."

Scripture Reading: Genesis 37:5-11

Key Lessons: Trusting and Obeying God Day by Day

We all have dreams and desires for the future. Sometimes it seems impossible for those dreams to become a reality. But when we delight ourselves in the LORD and commit our way to Him, He will do so much more for us than we ever thought possible. If we love spending time with God in prayer and in His Word, He will put His desires and dreams in our heart and will fulfill those dreams according to His perfect timing and will. Because Joseph led a life of obedience, God caused some amazing dreams that He had given Joseph to be fulfilled in his life. It wasn't easy, and it took a long time; but God did it:

Ge 37:5-11 "And Joseph dreamed a dream, and he told *it* his brethren: and they hated him yet the more. And he said unto them, Hear, I pray you, this dream which I have dreamed: For, behold, we *were* binding sheaves in the field, and, lo, my sheaf arose, and also stood upright; and, behold, your sheaves stood round about, and made obeisance to my sheaf. And his brethren said to him, Shalt thou indeed reign over us? or shalt thou indeed have dominion over us? And they hated him yet the more for his dreams, and for his words. And he dreamed yet another dream, and told it his brethren, and said, Behold, I have dreamed a dream more; and, behold, the sun and the moon and the eleven stars made obeisance to me. And he told *it* to his father, and to his brethren: and his father rebuked him, and said unto him, What *is* this dream that thou hast dreamed? Shall I and thy mother and thy brethren indeed come to bow down ourselves to thee to the earth? And his brethren envied him; but his father observed the saying."

As we mentioned, the dreams Joseph had were not ordinary dreams. They were dreams given to him by God that would be perfectly fulfilled. Through these dreams, God had put in Joseph's mind exactly what He was going to do for him and for his family in the future. Later, Joseph would tell Pharaoh, the king of Egypt, the same thing about his own dreams- that through them God was showing Pharaoh "what he *is* about to do" (Ge. 41:25).

Throughout the Old Testament, we find that God spoke to men through dreams. In Joseph's time, God's people did not have the written Word of God as we do today. The book of Job is thought to have been penned around the time of Abraham, so God's people may have had that part of God's written Word. But in that time, God spoke to men like Adam, Noah, Abraham, Isaac, Jacob, and other prophets directly or through visions and dreams. In Hebrews 1:1, the Bible tells us that God gave His word to the prophets of the Old Testament in many ways:

Heb 1:1-2 "God, who at sundry times and in divers manners spake in time past unto the fathers by the prophets, hath in these last days spoken unto us by *his* Son, whom he hath appointed heir of all things, by whom also he made the worlds."

So we see that in the days of the Old Testament when the Bible was not yet written down, God sometimes used visions and dreams to reveal His truth to His people. But in the New Testament time, He has revealed Himself to us through His Son, the Lord Jesus Christ. He has given us the complete written Word of God. **God speaks to us today through His Word, the Bible.** The prophets of the Old Testament received God's Word either directly or through dreams and visions, and then spoke forth God's word to the people. God showed these men what He was about to do and commanded them to tell it to others. This is what God did for Joseph through his dreams. He gave Joseph a vision of something that He was going to do in the future. Joseph took the dreams God gave him very seriously and eagerly told them to his brothers and to his father.

Joseph's first dream was about sheaves in a field. A sheaf is a bundle of grain. In Bible times, grain was cut with a sharp instrument called a scythe. The cut blades of grain were then gathered up by hand and tied in bundles, so that they could be carried and stored. In his dream, Joseph and his brothers were binding sheaves of grain into bundles. Joseph's sheaf rose up and stood upright. His brother's sheaves surrounded Joseph's and "made obeisance" to Joseph's sheaf. To make obeisance means to bow down and give honor to someone of great authority, such as a king.

A sheaf has no power to raise itself up or to bow down. It is an object, not a living thing. The fact that Joseph's sheaf rose up, is a picture of the fact that God would do this thing. Joseph would not raise himself up. God would raise Joseph up to a place of authority and power. When God raised Joseph up to this place, his brothers would be subject to him. It is also of interest that Joseph's first dream was about grain. As we will see, later in Joseph's life God would raise him up to be in charge of the food supply of the entire land of Egypt and of the whole world. People from all over the world would come to Joseph to buy grain- including his own brothers (Ge. 41:56-57). Even this detail is pictured in Joseph's dream of the sheaves.

God then gave Joseph a second dream. In this dream, the sun, the moon, and eleven stars bowed down to Joseph. This pictured the fact that Joseph's entire family would be made subject to him. This too came to pass in God's time. The fact that Joseph's dream was given to him in two different forms demonstrated the fact that God would certainly bring it to pass (Ge. 41:32).

Joseph was God's special servant. His dreams were not visions of his own mind. They were prophecies about the future. Later, God gave Joseph the ability to understand His will through the interpretation of important dreams that He gave to others. Joseph knew the dreams he had were special and that they were from God, so he shared them with his brothers and with his father, Jacob. Interestingly enough, God had once spoken to Joseph's father, Jacob, through a dream:

Ge 28:11-17 "And he [Jacob] lighted upon a certain place, and tarried there all night, because the sun was set; and he took of the stones of that place, and put *them for* his pillows, and lay down in that place to sleep. And he dreamed, and behold a ladder set up on the earth, and the top of it reached to heaven: and behold the angels of God ascending and descending on it. And, behold, the LORD stood above it, and said, I *am* the LORD God of Abraham thy father, and the God of Isaac: the land whereon thou liest, to thee will I give it, and to thy seed; And thy seed shall be as the dust of the earth, and thou shalt spread abroad to the west, and to the east, and to the north, and to the south: and in thee and in thy seed shall all the families of the earth be blessed. And, behold, I *am* with thee, and will keep thee in all *places* whither thou goest, and will bring thee again into this land; for I will not leave thee, until I have done *that* which I have spoken to thee of. And Jacob awaked out of his sleep, and he said, Surely the LORD is in this place; and I knew *it* not. And he was afraid, and said, How dreadful *is* this place! this *is* none other but the house of God, and this *is* the gate of heaven."

If anyone should understand the significance of God-given dreams, it was Joseph's father, Jacob. God had brought Jacob and his family back to the land He had promised to Abraham and Isaac. God had blessed Jacob with twelve sons and a daughter. He had already fulfilled some of the promises given to Jacob in his dream. God would fulfill all of His promises concerning Jacob's seed, and He would fulfill the pictures represented in Joseph's dreams as well.

Joseph eagerly shared what God had shown him in his dreams with his family; but like other prophets of the LORD who spoke forth God's Word, Joseph's dreams and his words were not well received. His brothers were furious that Joseph would imply that he would one day rule over them. Joseph was only telling them what God had shown him, but his brothers viewed it as arrogance. They hated Joseph more than ever- "for his dreams and for his words." They did not consider that Joseph was telling them God's truth. They thought Joseph was just bragging.

The same thing can happen to us when we speak forth the plain Word of God today. Sometimes people will hate us for speaking it. The Word of God shines light upon sin. We are only the messengers of God's Word, but people may accuse us of arrogance and pride for thinking we can be saved and forgiven, while they are condemned and still in their sins. We who are saved know that it is only by God's grace and His work on the cross that we can be called the children of God. We want others to know that they too can be forgiven if they will but come to Jesus Christ in repentance and faith. No one has to go to hell. People choose to go there because they will not go God's way through faith in Christ alone. Jesus told His disciples that they would be hated for His name's sake:

Joh 15:18-21 "If the world hate you, ye know that it hated me before *it hated* you. If ye were of the world, the world would love his own: but because ye are not of the world, but I have chosen you out of the world, therefore the world hateth you. Remember the word that I said unto you, The servant is not greater than his lord. If they have persecuted me, they will also persecute you; if they have kept my saying, they will keep yours also. But all these things will they do unto you for my name's sake, because they know not him that sent me."

Even other Christians who are not living in obedience to God may accuse us of pride or arrogance for having godly convictions. We must be careful to have a humble spirit, but we must also stand for right, even when others misunderstand. Sometimes we are guilty of pride. We need to be careful to humbly obey God and

His Word by His strength and with a right spirit. But we must never back down from doing what God commands, even when others may misunderstand or accuse us of wrong motives. All we have, even the strength and understanding to do what is right, comes from God.

Joseph's brothers could have experienced God's grace and blessing if they had listened to the LORD. Instead, they hated Joseph. Even Joseph's father rebuked him for implying that he and his mother and brothers would someday bow down to him. It was hard for a father to hear that he would bow before his own son. Yet, unlike Joseph's brethren, Jacob "observed the saying." He took what Joseph said seriously. Jacob knew that God had spoken to him in a dream. If these dreams were from the LORD, God would fulfill them. Jacob surely knew that Joseph's dreams would only stir up more strife with his brethren. But Jacob had seen too much of the hand of the LORD in his own life to cast Joseph's dreams aside as mere imagination. He knew they were significant, and took note of them in his heart.

Joseph's dreams fueled the fire of hatred already burning in the hearts of his brothers. That fire would bring awful consequences for all of them. For Joseph, it would bring suffering and persecution, but God's hand would purify Joseph through his trials and bring him to the place of God's perfect will. Joseph did not understand all that he would have to go through to see the fulfillment of the dreams that God gave him, but he committed his way to the Lord.

Personal Reflection:

Joseph would have to trust the Lord step by step. It's the same for us today. Often, we think of the will of God as something far out in the distant future; but the will of God is today. God wants to lead us to do His will now. God's will is as simple as spending time with Him each day and fulfilling our daily responsibilities with diligence and obedience. As we obey God, He will lead us step by step into the fulfillment of His perfect plan for our lives. On the other hand, if we go our own way, we will reap the fruit of our own doings- the fruit of sorrow, and bitterness, and regret. God's blessings are worth our obedience. Follow Him today. He is the Good Shepherd who will never lead us astray.

"My Shepherd Will Supply My Need"

My shepherd will supply my need:

Be An Example

Jehovah is His name;
In pastures fresh He makes me feed,
Beside the living stream.
He brings my wandering spirit back
When I forsake His ways,
And leads me, for His mercy's sake,
In paths of truth and grace.

When I walk through the shades of death
Thy presence is my stay;
One word of Thy supporting breath
Drives all my fears away.
Thy hand in sight of all my foes,
Doth still my table spread;
My cup with blessings overflows,
Thine oil anoints my head.

The sure provisions of my God
Attend me all my days;
O may Thy house be mine abode,
And all my work be praise!

There would I find a settled rest,
While others go and come;
No more a stranger, nor a guest,
But like a child at home.

-Isaac Watts, 1719

Chapter 8: "The Life of Joseph" (Part 3)

Memory Verses:

Ps 40:1-3 "I waited patiently for the LORD; and he inclined unto me, and heard my cry. He brought me up also out of an horrible pit, out of the miry clay, and set my feet upon a rock, *and* established my goings. And he hath put a new song in my mouth, *even* praise unto our God: many shall see *it*, and fear, and shall trust in the LORD."

Scripture Reading: Genesis 37:12-36

Key Lessons: Courageous obedience; Trusting God through trials

We all face trials and suffering in life. Sometimes our problems are a result of our own bad choices or sin in our lives. God chastens and corrects His children who are living in disobedience to Him. But why does God allow His obedient children to suffer? Sometimes it's hard to understand why God's people must suffer, but God always has a purpose in the things He allows in the lives of His children.

Be An Example

God uses trials to purify us and strengthen our faith if we allow Him to work through them. In fact, as we have learned even from our first lesson about the life of Abel, God's people often suffer because they are hated by those who do not love God and because we live in a sinful world in rebellion against God. Jesus said in John 16:33:

Joh 16:33 "These things I have spoken unto you, that in me ye might have peace. In the world ye shall have tribulation: but be of good cheer; I have overcome the world."

This will always be true as long as we live in this world and follow the Lord Jesus. In this world we will have trouble. But through dependence upon the Lord Jesus, we can still live in victory and peace- even in the midst of problems and suffering.

Joseph learned this lesson well. The trials he went through prepared him for the special work God had for him to do. Throughout the Word of God, we find that all of the great servants of God had to go through times of purifying and suffering to learn to trust God and to prepare them for God's work. Abraham and Sarah were tested for many years as they waited for the son God had promised them; Moses spent forty years in the wilderness before he was called to lead the children of Israel out of Egypt; David was a humble shepherd, then spent over twenty years running for his life from King Saul to prepare him to be the king of Israel. God prepares His servants to do His work through trials and often over long years of time. The same was true for Joseph. As a young person and as a man, he went through suffering and testing, but through it all, he trusted God. God wants us to submit to Him as Joseph did. He wants us to be ready to do His work in His time.

1Pe 1:7 "That the trial of your faith, being much more precious than of gold that perisheth, though it be tried with fire, might be found unto praise and honour and glory at the appearing of Jesus Christ:"

Jas 1:2-3 "My brethren, count it all joy when ye fall into divers temptations; Knowing *this*, that the trying of your faith worketh patience."

The Hatred of Joseph's Brothers:

One of the saddest trials Joseph had to endure was the hatred his brothers had for him. They saw him as an arrogant tattletale- the pet of their father. Their hatred became so deep, their bitterness so great that they sought an opportunity to kill him:

Ge 37:12-17 "And his brethren went to feed their father's flock in Shechem. And Israel said unto Joseph, Do not thy brethren feed *the flock* in Shechem? come, and I will send thee unto them. And he said to him, Here *am I*. And he said to him, Go, I pray thee, see whether it be well with thy brethren, and well with the flocks; and bring me word again. So he sent him out of the vale of Hebron, and he came to Shechem. And a certain man found him, and, behold, *he was* wandering in the field: and the man asked him, saying, What seekest thou? And he said, I seek my brethren: tell me, I pray thee, where they feed *their flocks*. And the man said, They are departed hence; for I heard them say, Let us go to Dothan. And Joseph went after his brethren, and found them in Dothan."

Joseph's Submission to His Father:

Israel and his sons were nomadic shepherds in Canaan. When the pasture grass was eaten in one place, the shepherds would take the flocks to new places to graze. Joseph's brothers had gone to Shechem to feed their flocks. Israel wanted Joseph to go and see how his brothers were doing and to bring him word again. Israel may have been concerned about their safety or the state of the flocks, but sadly, he also knew he couldn't trust his other sons to do what was right. Joseph had been the bearer of bad tidings about his brothers' behavior before. Israel knew he could trust Joseph to see if things were as they should be. Though Joseph was the youngest, he was the most trusted of Israel's sons. This definitely didn't put Joseph in good favor with his older brothers, but it was the truth.

Joseph's response to his father showed both courage and obedience. He said, "Here am I." Joseph was ready to obey and to do whatever his father asked him to do. We see again how much Joseph was a picture of the Lord Jesus Christ. In everything, Christ did the will of His Father- even in coming from Heaven to earth to be the Lamb of God and to be sacrificed for the sins of the world. Joseph too, was willing to do the will of his father even when it meant leaving the place of safety with his father who loved him, to go seek his brethren who hated and despised him. The Bible says that Israel sent Joseph "out of the vale of Hebron" to Shechem. A vale is a valley between two hills or mountains. It is a place of safety and security. Joseph had great courage to do what his father asked. That's what obedience requires- courage to do what is right even when others may hate us for it. Joseph left the safety and security of Hebron to go alone to seek his brothers.

But when he came to the place where his brothers should have been, they were nowhere to be found.

The Perseverance of Joseph:

Joseph ran into an obstacle. He couldn't find his brothers, but he didn't give up and say, "Oh well, I tried," and return home. He stayed and searched, and as he was wondering what to do, God provided the answer. As Joseph was wandering in the field, a "certain man" found him and told him where his brethren had gone. God sent this man to guide Joseph. When we obey the Lord, we can expect to run into obstacles too, but that is never the time to quit. We must persevere and keep following the Lord's leading, and He will show us what to do in His time. Joseph's brothers had gone to a place called Dothan. Joseph had already travelled from thirty to fifty miles from Hebron to Shechem. Dothan was another eight to ten miles north. No doubt it was a weary journey for Joseph, but he did not hesitate to fulfill the purpose for which his father had sent him- to find his brethren. Finally, he came upon them in Dothan.

Joseph's Brothers Conspire Against Him:

Ge 37:18 -20 "And when they saw him afar off, even before he came near unto them, they conspired against him to slay him. And they said one to another, Behold, this dreamer cometh. Come now therefore, and let us slay him, and cast him into some pit, and we will say, Some evil beast hath devoured him: and we shall see what will become of his dreams."

When Joseph's brothers saw him coming, they began to scoff at him, "Behold this dreamer cometh." They did not consider that Joseph's dreams were from God. They foolishly thought they could stop the fulfillment of God's plan by killing Joseph. They said "let us slay him...and we shall see what will become of his dreams." No plan can succeed against the Lord. God would fulfill His plan through Joseph just as He promised.

The Bible warns against being a scoffer- a mocker of God and of His truth. Psalm 1:1 says, "Blessed *is* the man that walketh not in the counsel of the ungodly, nor standeth in the way of sinners, nor sitteth in the seat of the scornful." Joseph's brothers were scornful. They scoffed at God's truth in Joseph's dreams and were murderers in their hearts. They were like those described in Proverbs 1 who conspire together to murder the innocent. In this case, the innocent one they wanted to kill was their own brother:

Pr 1:10-12 "My son, if sinners entice thee, consent thou not. If they say, Come with us, let us lay wait for blood, let us lurk privily for the innocent without cause: Let us swallow them up alive as the grave; and whole, as those that go down into the pit:"

Joseph's Brothers' Plan to Hide Their Sin:

Joseph's brothers not only made up a plan to kill their brother, they also made a plan to cover up the murder. They said, "Come now therefore, and let us slay him, and cast him into some pit, and we will say, Some evil beast hath devoured him..." Remember, God's Word warns us about the foolishness of trying to cover sin. Sin will always come out, either in this life or in the life to come (1 Ti. 5:24). The Bible says in Proverbs 28:13, "He that covereth his sins shall not prosper..." and in Numbers 32:23, it says "...be sure your sin will find you out." Joseph's brothers were deceived to think they could kill their brother and get away with it. They may hide it from their father, but they could not hide it from God. God knew the hatred in their hearts. He knew their plan even before they spoke the words. We cannot hide our sins either. God sees all that we do. He hears all that we say, and He understands every thought of our hearts. We may hide things from our parents, our spouse, or others, but we cannot hide from God:

Heb 4:13 "Neither is there any creature that is not manifest in his sight: but all things *are* naked and opened unto the eyes of him with whom we have to do."

Ec 12:14 "For God shall bring every work into judgment, with every secret thing, whether *it be* good, or whether *it be* evil."

Ps 90:8 "Thou hast set our iniquities before thee, our secret *sins* in the light of thy countenance."

We must not be deceived as Joseph's brothers were. Though man may not see what we do; though our parents may not see, God sees, and we will answer to Him.

Reuben Saves Joseph from Death:

Ge 37:21-24 "And Reuben heard *it*, and he delivered him out of their hands; and said, Let us not kill him. And Reuben said unto them, Shed no blood, *but* cast him into this pit that *is* in the wilderness, and lay no hand upon him; that he might rid him out of their hands, to deliver him to his father again. And it came to pass, when Joseph was come unto his brethren, that they stript Joseph out of his coat, *his* coat of *many* colours that *was* on him; And they took him, and cast him into a pit: and the pit *was* empty, *there was* no water in it."

Reuben was the oldest of Jacob's sons, the firstborn of his wife, Leah. He heard his brothers plotting to kill Joseph and intervened to save Joseph's life. Reuben convinced his brothers to throw Joseph into a pit rather than killing him outright. He planned to take Joseph out later and return him back to his father. Since he was the eldest, Reuben would certainly be held the most responsible by his father if anything happened to Joseph. Also, Reuben had already dishonored his father in an earlier incident in Genesis 35 when he had committed immorality with his father's own wife, Bilhah. Reuben was not in good standing with his Dad. Whatever his motives were, Reuben was right to want to save Joseph, but he went about it the wrong way. He knew the vicious hatred of his brothers for Joseph, so he decided to go along with them to a point, and then try to save Joseph secretly in the end. He tried to save Joseph's life by playing both sides.

This is a temptation for us as well, and it is so prevalent in Christianity today. We feel that if we can compromise with the world we can win more people to Christ; but true Christianity doesn't work that way. True Christianity reflects the holy God of Heaven and is a work of the Holy Spirit of God. We can't accomplish God's plan through human, carnal methods. Reuben thought he had a good plan, but it was doomed to failure. Sometimes we think a little compromise with what is wrong is okay as long as something good is accomplished in the end. But it never works out that way. Compromising with sin always results in sorrow, heartbreak, and failure. We cannot stand for God and compromise with sin at the same time.

Jas 4:4 "... know ye not that the friendship of the world is enmity with God? whosoever therefore will be a friend of the world is the enemy of God."

Later in this same passage in James, the Bible tells us:

Jas 4:7-8 "Submit yourselves therefore to God. Resist the devil, and he will flee from you. Draw nigh to God, and he will draw nigh to you. Cleanse *your* hands, *ye* sinners; and purify *your* hearts, *ye* double minded."

Reuben's problem was that he was double minded. He thought he could go along with his wicked brothers and please his father at the same time. Reuben's plan would ultimately fail to return Joseph to his father, and it would cause untold suffering for Joseph.

The whole discussion about murdering Joseph and then Reuben's plan to throw him into a pit instead took place as the brothers watched Joseph come to them from afar off. By the time Joseph reached them, there was no turning back. Their malice boiled over. They seized Joseph and stripped him of his coat- the hated symbol of their father's special love. The stripping of Joseph's coat is a picture of Christ's suffering and separation from His Father as He took our sins upon Himself. Christ willingly gave Himself up to be mercilessly mistreated at the hands of sinners. He was stripped of His robe and brutally mocked, beaten, and nailed to a cross. As He hung upon the cross the Bible says that He "became sin for us who knew no sin; that we might be made the righteousness of God in him" (2 Co. 5:21). Christ was stripped of His Father's love as the wrath of God was poured out upon Him for our sakes. Jesus was the innocent Lamb of God slain in the place of sinners. Like Christ, Joseph was stripped of his robe, the symbol of his father's love, and separated from his father by the wicked hatred of his brothers.

Joseph's brothers threw him into a nearby pit. The pit was an empty cistern- a large hole for collecting rainwater in the wilderness. The cistern was empty at the time, and Reuben thought that throwing Joseph in there would give him time to save him and take him back to his father at some point. But Reuben was going to find that trying to play both sides of right and wrong doesn't work out well. He happened to be away from camp- perhaps taking his turn watching the flocks or some other errand -when his brothers changed the plan. While Reuben was away, they seized upon an opportunity to get rid of Joseph once and for all- without his blood upon their hands and with profit to boot -or so they thought. After throwing their younger brother into the pit, they callously sat down to eat. It was then that they saw something approaching in the distance:

Ge 37:25-36 "And they sat down to eat bread: and they lifted up their eyes and looked, and, behold, a company of Ishmeelites came from Gilead with their camels bearing spicery and balm and myrrh, going to carry *it* down to Egypt. And Judah said unto his brethren, What profit *is it* if we slay our brother, and conceal his blood? Come, and let us sell him to the Ishmeelites, and let not our hand be upon him; for he *is* our brother *and* our flesh. And his brethren were content. Then there passed by Midianites merchantmen; and they drew and lifted up Joseph out of the pit, and sold Joseph to the Ishmeelites for twenty *pieces* of silver: and they brought Joseph into Egypt. And Reuben returned unto the pit; and, behold, Joseph *was* not in the pit; and he rent his clothes. And he returned unto his brethren, and said, The child *is* not; and I, whither shall I go? And they took Joseph's coat, and killed a kid of the goats, and dipped the coat in the blood; And they sent the coat of *many* colours, and they brought *it* to their father; and said, This have we found: know now whether it *be* thy son's coat or no. And he knew it, and said, *It is* my son's coat; an evil beast hath devoured him; Joseph is without doubt rent in pieces. And Jacob rent his clothes, and put sackcloth upon his loins, and mourned for his son many days. And all his sons and all his daughters rose up to comfort him; but he refused to be comforted; and he said, For I will go down into the grave unto my son mourning. Thus his father wept for him. And the Midianites sold him into Egypt unto Potiphar, an officer of Pharaoh's, *and* captain of the guard."

Joseph's brethren saw some Ishmaelite and Midianite merchants travelling to Egypt. On Judah's suggestion, they sold Joseph as a slave to them for twenty pieces of silver. The brothers thought they could be rid of Joseph without killing him themselves. When Reuben returned to save his brother out of the pit, Joseph was gone. Reuben was devastated. He knew this would be the last straw for him with his father. This is shown in his reaction, "The child is not; and I, whither shall I go?" Rather than returning and telling his father the truth, Reuben joined with his brothers in covering their sin. They took Joseph's coat and dipped it in goat's blood and took it back to their father. They lied and said they "found" it. They knew what their father would think- that Joseph had been torn to pieces and killed by a wild animal. This cowardly act of the sons of Israel was crueler than the truth. They caused their father to think that his beloved son was dead when they had really sold him into slavery themselves. They watched in wicked silence as their father mourned for Joseph. Covering sin always brings awful consequences. For years, the sons of Israel would live with the guilt of what they had done while they watched their father mourn and suffer. Joseph would also suffer because of the wickedness of his brothers, but God would bless him wherever he went. God was directing Joseph's steps even through his trials. He would never leave or forsake Joseph. Joseph had the peace of knowing he was in God's hands and in His will.

<u>Personal Reflection:</u>

We find from this chapter in Joseph's life the danger of compromising with sin. We also learn the heartbreak of hiding sin. Is there some area of your life in which you are compromising with what is wrong? Is there some hidden sin in your life that you need to make right with God? Remember, the Lord has mercy when we are willing to be honest with Him.

We also learn how God uses trials in our lives to accomplish His purpose. If you are going through hard times, ask the Lord to search your heart to be certain your problems are not caused by some sin or bad habit in your life. Then commit your way to the Lord. Ask Him to help you to do right, even through the hard times. Like Joseph, God wants to use the hard times to make you more like Him and to prepare you to do His will. God cares about our heartaches and sorrows. He can give comfort even when we feel completely alone. He will never leave us or forsake us.

"Be Still My Soul"

Be still, my soul: the Lord is on thy side.
Bear patiently the cross of grief or pain.
Leave to thy God to order and provide;
In every change, He faithful will remain.
Be still, my soul: thy best, thy heav'nly Friend
Through thorny ways leads to a joyful end.

Be still, my soul: thy God doth undertake
To guide the future, as He has the past.
Thy hope, thy confidence let nothing shake;
All now mysterious shall be bright at last.
Be still, my soul: the waves and winds still know
His voice Who ruled them while He dwelt below.

Be still, my soul: when dearest friends depart,
And all is darkened in the vale of tears,

Be An Example

Then shalt thou better know His love, His heart,
Who comes to soothe thy sorrow and thy fears.
Be still, my soul: thy Jesus can repay
From His own fullness all He takes away.

Be still, my soul: the hour is hast'ning on
When we shall be forever with the Lord.
When disappointment, grief, and fear are gone,
Sorrow forgot, love's purest joys restored.
Be still, my soul: when change and tears are past
All safe and blessed we shall meet at last.

Be still, my soul: begin the song of praise
On earth, believing, to Thy Lord on high;
Acknowledge Him in all thy words and ways,
So shall He view thee with a well-pleased eye.
Be still, my soul: the Sun of life divine
Through passing clouds shall but more brightly shine.

-Katharina A. von Schlegel, 1752

Chapter 9: "The Life of Joseph" (Part 4)

Memory Verse:

Php 4:8 "Finally, brethren, whatsoever things are true, whatsoever things *are* honest, whatsoever things *are* just, whatsoever things *are* pure, whatsoever things *are* lovely, whatsoever things *are* of good report; if *there be* any virtue, and if *there be* any praise, think on these things."

Ps 119:9-11 "Wherewithal shall a young man cleanse his way? by taking heed *thereto* according to thy word. With my whole heart have I sought thee: O let me not wander from thy commandments. Thy word have I hid in mine heart, that I might not sin against thee."

Scripture Reading: Genesis 39

Key Lessons: Keeping a pure heart; fleeing temptation

Purity means to be clean- to be free from the guilt of sin. As a Christian, this should be the goal for our lives. We all need constant cleansing from sin, but our daily habits and thoughts will determine whether sin will take root in our lives. Sin always begins in the heart. What we put into our minds is very important- television, books, movies, video games, music -all of these things can pollute our minds if we're not careful to measure our activities by God's Word. Philippians 4:8, one of our memory verses, is so important, for it gives us a true guide to examine our lives in the light of God's Word:

Is what I'm doing consistent with God's truth? Is it honest before God and men? Is it fair and just? Is it morally pure? Is it of lovely character in God's eyes? Is it of good report- something that contributes to a good testimony? Is it something that promotes virtue and praise to God? So many of the things that permeate our worldly culture do not stand up to these tests of God's Word and should not be part of a Christian's life. Rather, we should fill our minds and hearts with God's Word and with music that reflects the character of the Holy Spirit of God.

Psalm 119 also gives us the key to a pure life- obeying God's Word and seeking Him daily in prayer. How can we be clean before God? By taking heed to God's

Word and obeying His commandments- by seeking God with our whole heart. Oh, what joy there is in obeying God's Word! There is such peace in knowing we are right before Him. Putting God's Word into our hearts will strengthen us to do what is right when the tests come.

Joseph was an example of someone who stayed pure before God even in the worst of circumstances. In Genesis 39, Joseph faced a very difficult test in the area of moral purity. Joseph had prepared his heart in advance to obey the Lord, and through faith and obedience to God's truth, Joseph passed the test.

Joseph was sold as a slave to Ishmaelite traders by his own brothers. He was forcibly taken from his home and his dear father; but even in these horrible circumstances, Joseph was ever in God's care.

God's Care for Joseph:

Genesis 39:1-3 "And Joseph was brought down to Egypt; and Potiphar, an officer of Pharaoh, captain of the guard, an Egyptian, bought him of the hands of the Ishmeelites, which had brought him down thither. And the LORD was with Joseph, and he was a prosperous man; and he was in the house of his master the Egyptian. "

Joseph was taken far from his home to the land of Egypt. The trip to Egypt would not have been a pleasant one for Joseph. He was treated in every way as a slave. In fact, the book of Psalms tells us some specific things about Joseph's suffering during this time:

Ps 105:17-18 "He sent a man before them, *even* Joseph, *who* was sold for a servant: Whose feet they hurt with fetters: he was laid in iron:"

Joseph's feet were put in fetters. Fetters were metal cuffs connected with a chain that were put around a prisoner's ankles and sometimes around their wrists to prevent them from escaping. The metal on these cuffs would cut through the skin and make it very difficult to walk. They were made of iron, so they were heavy as well. Joseph was put in fetters of iron.

The trip from Canaan to Egypt would have been well over two hundred miles. Imagine the misery of walking through the wilderness for that distance while bound with iron fetters under the tyranny of cruel men- and all along the way to suffer hunger, thirst, weariness, and abuse. Joseph suffered all of these things, as well as the emotional anguish of being separated from his beloved father because of the wicked treachery and hatred of his own brothers. All that was precious in this world was taken from Joseph in an instant all because he had obeyed his father.

In spite of all these circumstances, the Bible tells us that "the LORD was with Joseph." God had not forsaken him. God had prepared a man named Potiphar to buy Joseph who would show great kindness to him. Potiphar was a very powerful and wealthy man. He was the captain of Pharaoh's guard- the head over the prison where political prisoners were held (Ge. 40:7); and as such, he was responsible for the safety and security of Pharaoh himself. Joseph became a servant in the house of this powerful and influential man. No doubt Potiphar had many slaves who worked on his property and in his fields, but Joseph was chosen to be a house servant and eventually rose to the highest position in Potiphar's house. God blessed Joseph for his faithfulness. Though his circumstances were difficult, God's hand was upon him in everything he did. The Bible tells us that Joseph was "a prosperous man." Imagine that! Even as a slave, God caused Joseph to be prosperous. He was successful in everything he did. The Bible tells us the secret to success in Psalm 1:1-3:

Ps 1:1-3 "Blessed *is* the man that walketh not in the counsel of the ungodly, nor standeth in the way of sinners, nor sitteth in the seat of the scornful. But his delight *is* in the law of the LORD; and in his law doth he meditate day and night. And he shall be like a tree planted by the rivers of water, that bringeth forth his fruit in his season; his leaf also shall not wither; and whatsoever he doeth shall prosper."

This was Joseph's testimony. He did not walk in the counsel of the ungodly. He did not take the advice of ungodly people or take part with those who acted wickedly and scorned the truth of God- even when the scorners were his own brothers. Instead, Joseph delighted in obeying God's Word. He thought upon God's truth day and night. This was the secret to Joseph's success. This can be your testimony too. It is a choice to obey God and to refuse to join with wickedness. Because Joseph made this choice, God blessed him with great prosperity even as a slave in Egypt.

Joseph's Faithful Testimony before Potiphar:

Ge 39:4-6 "And his master saw that the LORD *was* with him, and that the LORD made all that he did to prosper in his hand. And Joseph found grace in his sight, and he served him: and he made him overseer over his house, and all *that* he had he put into his hand. And it came to pass from the time *that* he had made him overseer in his house, and over all that he had, that the LORD blessed the Egyptian's house for Joseph's sake; and the blessing of the LORD was upon all that he had in the house, and in the field. And he left all that he had in Joseph's hand; and he knew not ought he had, save the bread which he did eat. And Joseph was *a* goodly *person*, and well favoured."

The LORD caused Potiphar to notice Joseph's competence and trustworthiness. God's blessing was upon Joseph in such a way that Potiphar could not help but see it. Potiphar saw "that the LORD was with" Joseph, and "that the LORD made all that he did to prosper in his hand." The Egyptians had many false gods that they worshipped, but they knew of the God of Abraham. Joseph "found grace" in his master's sight. The word "grace" means favor. Joseph found favor in the eyes of his master and was promoted to be the overseer over Potiphar's entire household and all that he had. In fact, with Joseph in charge, Potiphar knew he didn't have to worry about anything. God blessed Potiphar in a special way because God's man, Joseph, was his overseer. Everything in his house and in his fields prospered under Joseph's care. This was a wonderful time for Joseph to serve the Lord with a good testimony before his master, and it was a wonderful time for Potiphar to enjoy and to see the blessings of the true God.

The Bible tells us another thing about Joseph in these verses. It says that Joseph was "a goodly person, and well favoured." This description refers to Joseph's physical appearance. Joseph was a handsome young man and favorable to look upon. This too was God's blessing upon Joseph, but unfortunately, Potiphar was not the only one to notice this about Joseph. Potiphar's wife, an adulterous woman, noticed it too.

Ge 39:7-10 "And it came to pass after these things, that his master's wife cast her eyes upon Joseph; and she said, Lie with me. But he refused, and said unto his master's wife, Behold, my master wotteth not what *is* with me in the house, and he hath committed all that he hath to my hand; *There is* none greater in this house than I; neither hath he kept back any thing from me but thee, because thou *art* his wife: how then can I do this great wickedness, and sin against God? And it came to pass, as she spake to Joseph day by day, that he hearkened not unto her, to lie by her, *or* to be with her.”

Potiphar's Wicked Wife:

Potiphar had a wicked, immoral wife. She “cast her eyes upon Joseph.” She noticed that Joseph was a handsome man, and, though she was a married woman, she invited Joseph to “lie with her.” This is what the Bible calls adultery. God's Word teaches us that physical intimacy between a man and a woman is a privilege to be enjoyed only within marriage. In fact, the Bible tells us in 1 Corinthians 7:1-2 that the way for a Christian man to stay pure is not to touch a woman, but rather to have his own wife.

1Co 7:1-2 “Now concerning the things whereof ye wrote unto me: *It is* good for a man not to touch a woman. Nevertheless, *to avoid* fornication, let every man have his own wife, and let every woman have her own husband.”

In our culture today, we are constantly bombarded by sensual images and the false notion that staying pure until marriage is old fashioned. Young people are encouraged by movies, television, music, friends, etc., that it is normal to fulfill impure desires before marriage with whomever they choose. Adults are encouraged to be unfaithful to their spouses and to fulfill their lusts however they please as well. But God's Word has not changed. In fact, the Word of God tells Christians very plainly to stay pure and to flee youthful lusts. Sensual desire is a physical drive, much like hunger and thirst. We have to decide in advance to stay pure and depend upon the Lord's strength. The Bible says,

2Ti 2:22 “Flee also youthful lusts: but follow righteousness, faith, charity, peace, with them that call on the Lord out of a pure heart.”

As Christians, we are to flee from youthful lusts- to run away from them. We are not to stay in situations where we will be tempted to sin. Also, we are to fellowship with other Christians who “call on the Lord out of a pure heart.” If we stay away from the wrong company and fellowship with faithful Christians who have pure hearts, we will save ourselves from many of the situations that bring sensual temptations. When those temptations come without our consent, we must not stay in the place of temptation, but run from it. Sin often takes hold upon us gradually. We give in little by little, and before long, it's too late. That's why, when it comes to physical purity, God has set the boundary for our greatest safety in 1 Corinthians 7 and has given us the defense against that temptation in 2 Timothy 2:22: "Flee youthful lusts." We find that is exactly what Joseph did.

Joseph's Faithful Obedience:

Joseph immediately refused the request of Potiphar's wife and gave a godly reason for doing so. She was his master's wife. Potiphar had entrusted him with all that he had and had shown him great kindness. He would not do such a thing to Potiphar, but more importantly, Joseph would not do "this great wickedness and sin against God." Joseph called the sin that Potiphar's wife offered him what it was – "great wickedness." This is something we need to remember when temptation comes. Sin is an offence against the God of Heaven. Joseph loved God. He could not do this thing and sin against the LORD. Potiphar's wife, unlike Joseph, had no fear of the God of Heaven. She would not give up easily. She was determined to wear Joseph down to have her wicked way.

Ge 39:7-12 " And it came to pass, as she spake to Joseph day by day, that he hearkened not unto her, to lie by her, *or* to be with her. And it came to pass about this time, that *Joseph* went into the house to do his business; and *there was* none of the men of the house there within. And she caught him by his garment, saying, Lie with me: and he left his garment in her hand, and fled, and got him out."

The temptation Joseph faced did not happen just once. Potiphar's wife came to Joseph again and again, pressing him to lie with her and to sin against the LORD. Joseph acted with wisdom. He knew that temptation would overcome him if he was not careful, so, he not only refused her; he avoided her as much as possible. The day finally came, however, when things came to a crisis point. Joseph was doing his master's business in the house, and the other men of the house were all out doing other things. Potiphar's wife saw this as her golden opportunity. She grabbed Joseph by his garment and said again, "Lie with me." Joseph did not stay around to allow her to get close to him or affect his passions. Instead, he left his garment in her hand and fled and "got him out."

This is exactly what the Bible tells us to do in the face of lustful temptation -flee. Unfortunately for Joseph, Potiphar's wife was not only an adulteress. She was a liar. Joseph had rejected her for the last time. Now, she would have her revenge.

Joseph Falsely Accused :

Ge 39:13-20 "And it came to pass, when she saw that he had left his garment in her hand, and was fled forth, That she called unto the men of her house, and spake unto them, saying, See, he hath brought in an Hebrew unto us to mock us; he came in unto me to lie with me, and I cried with a loud voice: And it came to pass, when he heard that I lifted up my voice and cried, that he left his garment with me, and fled, and got him out. And she laid up his garment by her, until his lord came home. And she spake unto him according to these words, saying, The Hebrew servant, which thou hast brought unto us, came in unto me to mock me: And it came to pass, as I lifted up my voice and cried, that he left his garment with me, and fled out. And it came to pass, when his master heard the words of his wife, which she spake unto him, saying, After this manner did thy servant to me; that his wrath was kindled. And Joseph's master took him, and put him into the prison, a place where the king's prisoners *were* bound: and he was there in the prison."

Potiphar's wife completely turned the story around. She told the men of her house and her husband that Joseph had tried to force her to lie with him. She even cast a racial slur at Joseph, pointing to the fact that he was "an Hebrew." She had his garment to prove that all that she said was true. All the evidence pointed to Joseph's guilt. Potiphar's wrath was kindled- after all he had done for Joseph, after all he had trusted him with, now he would betray his trust and try to take his wife? Potiphar had Joseph put in the king's prison. He was left there- again in chains -though he had done no wrong. Poor Joseph-all the good testimony he had with his master was seemingly ruined by the lies of Potiphar's wicked wife.

God is Still Faithful:

This is one of the hardest things to endure- false accusation -to have our testimony hurt by lies and slander when we have tried to do right. It is easy in such circumstances to become bitter against those who have persecuted us. We might be tempted to despair and think, "What's the use of doing right?" How hard it must have been for Joseph. But he did not despair. He did not become bitter. Joseph knew it was right to obey God, regardless of the cost. God would make it right in the end. And God will do the same for us if we trust Him and obey. The Bible tells us that the godly in Christ Jesus will suffer in this world, but He has promised to be with us always. This was true for Joseph. In spite of everything, even in prison, God was with Joseph. God had not forgotten him or the dreams He had given him, and God would keep His promises.

Ge 39:21 "But the LORD was with Joseph, and shewed him mercy, and gave him favour in the sight of the keeper of the prison."

Once again, the LORD showed Joseph mercy and gave him favor in the sight of the keeper of the prison. God would use Joseph in a mighty way, even in this dark place.

Personal Reflection:

Are you going through adversity or temptation? God can give you strength to obey Him even in the hardest times. Are there things in your life that need to go- things that are not pure, or lovely, or of a good report? What we put in our hearts will come out. We need to fill our minds with God's Word and with sweet, godly music. We need to get rid of things that fill our minds with temptation and things that are not true. We also need to be careful to choose godly friends to associate with- those that love God and want to please Him. Then when temptation comes, we can do as Joseph did -flee from it.

1Co 10:13 "There hath no temptation taken you but such as is common to man: but God *is* faithful, who will not suffer you to be tempted above that ye are able; but will with the temptation also make a way to escape, that ye may be able to bear it."

"Yield Not to Temptation"

Yield not to temptation, for yielding is sin;
Each vict'ry will help you some other to win;
Fight manfully onward, dark passions subdue;
Look ever to Jesus, He will carry you through.

Refrain:
Ask the Savior to help you,
Comfort, strengthen, and keep you;
He is willing to aid you,
He will carry you through.

Shun evil companions, bad language disdain,
God's name hold in rev'rence, nor take it in vain;
Be thoughtful and earnest, kindhearted and true;
Look ever to Jesus, He will carry you through.

To him that o'ercometh, God giveth a crown,
Through faith we will conquer, though often cast down;
He who is our Savior, our strength will renew;
Look ever to Jesus, He will carry you through.

-Horatio R. Palmer, 1868

Be An Example

Chapter 10: "The Life of Joseph" (Part 5)

Memory verse:

Ps 37:7-9 "Rest in the LORD, and wait patiently for him: fret not thyself because of him who prospereth in his way, because of the man who bringeth wicked devices to pass. Cease from anger, and forsake wrath: fret not thyself in any wise to do evil. For evildoers shall be cut off: but those that wait upon the LORD, they shall inherit the earth."

Scripture Reading: Genesis 40

Key Lessons: Patience and trusting God through trials

Joseph would learn this lesson well- to wait upon God and rest in Him even when everything seemed hopeless. He had obeyed God and fled from temptation when Potiphar's wife tried to lure him to sin against the LORD. He was cast into prison because she falsely accused him of doing wrong. Everything looked dark for Joseph, but God had not forsaken him:

Ge 39:21-23 "But the LORD was with Joseph, and shewed him mercy, and gave him favour in the sight of the keeper of the prison. And the keeper of the prison committed to Joseph's hand all the prisoners that *were* in the prison; and whatsoever they did there, he was the doer *of it*. The keeper of the prison looked not to anything *that was* under his hand; because the LORD was with him, and *that* which he did, the LORD made *it* to prosper."

These verses are a testimony of God's faithfulness. God was with Joseph and blessed him- even in prison. These verses also show us the steadfast character of Joseph. He certainly could have been discouraged at this point. He could have given up on obeying God in such difficult circumstances and said, "What's the use of trying?" But he didn't. He knew it was right to obey God no matter what came. Because Joseph was a responsible and obedient young man, the warden put him in charge of the entire prison. Joseph could be trusted to do what was right, even when no one else was watching him. When he saw something that needed to be done, he did it. Because of his good testimony, the keeper of the prison trusted Joseph. He didn't even need to check on him. What a testimony Joseph had! He lived his life every day to obey God and to do his best.

What about us today? Can we be trusted to do our work at home or at school or at church even without being told? Do we do our best even when we're going through trials and problems? Joseph didn't complain about his circumstances. Instead, he committed his way to the Lord and did what was right. God can open up many blessings for us if we, like Joseph, will do what is right even in depressing circumstances. Because of his obedience and right attitude, God caused everything that Joseph did to prosper.

God Fulfills His Plan and Promise to Joseph Step by Step:

Remember the dreams that God had given to Joseph? He was only seventeen years old when God showed him that one day he would be exalted to a place of honor and authority even over his own family. Eleven years had passed since that time. Joseph was twenty eight years old. In that span of time he had been twice sold as a slave, then falsely accused, and cast into prison for a sin he did not commit. God hadn't forgotten the promises He had given Joseph in those dreams. He would bring it all to pass. In fact, God would use the unusual dreams of some other men to fulfill His plan for Joseph and for the entire world.

The Chief Butler and the Chief Baker's Troubling Dreams:

Ge 40:1-4 "And it came to pass after these things, *that* the butler of the king of Egypt and *his* baker had offended their lord the king of Egypt. And Pharaoh was wroth against two *of* his officers, against the chief of the butlers, and against the chief of the bakers. And he put them in ward in the house of the captain of the guard, into the prison, the place where Joseph *was* bound. And the captain of the guard charged Joseph with them, and he served them: and they continued a season in ward."

The chief butler and the chief baker were very high ranking officials in Pharaoh's household. The chief butler waited upon the king personally. He was responsible to give the king his wine in his royal cup. The chief baker was in charge of the very bread that the king ate. These men would have been some of the most trusted of all the king's servants. Something very serious must have happened to cause Pharaoh to cast these servants into prison. The Bible says that Pharaoh was wroth against them. Whatever they had been accused of, it was a personal affront to the king himself. They were not ordinary prisoners. They were put into the house of the captain of the guard- the special part of the prison where the king's prisoners were bound. When they were brought into the prison, the captain of the guard put Joseph in charge of them.

While these men were serving their term and awaiting their sentence, Joseph took care of their needs. All of this was part of God's plan for Joseph. What happened next was another step toward the fulfillment of the dreams God had given Joseph so many years before:

Ge 40:5-8 "And they dreamed a dream both of them, each man his dream in one night, each man according to the interpretation of his dream, the butler and the baker of the king of Egypt, which *were* bound in the prison. And Joseph came in unto them in the morning, and looked upon them, and, behold, they *were* sad. And he asked Pharaoh's officers that *were* with him in the ward of his lord's house, saying, Wherefore look ye *so* sadly to day? And they said unto him, We have dreamed a dream, and *there is* no interpreter of it. And Joseph said unto them, *Do* not interpretations *belong* to God? tell me *them*, I pray you."

Both of these men had unusual dreams on the same night. They knew they were not ordinary dreams, but surely had some supernatural significance. Their lives were already in the balance by being out of favor with the king. Death could descend upon them at any moment. When they had these dreams, their fears were multiplied. What was going to happen to them? They had been under Joseph's care for a while, since the Bible says they "continued a season in ward." Throughout this time, Joseph had faithfully served them. When Joseph came in to check on the men that day, he saw that they were sad about something. Joseph was concerned and asked them, "Wherefore look ye so sadly today?"

This teaches us something else about Joseph. Joseph cared for the troubles and needs of others. When he saw that the men were sad, he wanted to help. Are we like Joseph in this way? When we see someone sad or alone are we willing to go to them and try to help and comfort them? This is what God wants us to do. Sometimes we allow shyness or pride to keep us from reaching out. It's easier to stay comfortable where we are or to do what we want to do instead of taking the time to help someone who is hurting. But God wants us to care for the people that He brings into our lives. There are many ways we can show we care. Time is one of the most precious ways we can show our love. Just spending time talking with someone shows that we care about them. Many people are very lonely. They just want someone to listen to their problems and to be a friend to them. They need someone to pray with them. You can be that friend to others. What about those who are different from us? What about elderly people in our church or perhaps other young people who have special problems- are we willing to reach out to them? How about new people who come to our church or people in our neighborhood? Are we willing to speak to them and to make them feel loved? God has a ministry for each one of us, if we are willing to listen to His voice and obey Him when He tells us to reach out.

Php 2:4 says, "Look not every man on his own things, but every man also on the things of others."

God wants us to get our eyes off of ourselves and our own problems and to consider the needs of others- whoever they may be. This is what Joseph did. What would have happened if Joseph had not cared enough to ask these men what was troubling them? He may have missed what God wanted Him to do. We need to ask God to help us to be sensitive to the needs of others and to act on their behalf. God can use us- if we are willing to care and to help.

Thankfully, Joseph did care. When he asked these men why they were so sad, they told Joseph that they had each dreamed a dream, but had no one to interpret it. These were pagan men who worshipped the false gods of the Egyptians. As we will see in a later passage, when the Egyptian people had strange dreams, they did not look to the true God for help. Instead, they called upon "magicians" to interpret their dreams. These magicians used witchcraft and pagan rituals to try to find answers. Their interpretations were based upon the lies of the devil. This situation with the butler and the baker opened the door for Joseph to tell them about the true God of Heaven. Joseph said, "Do not interpretations belong to God? Tell me them, I pray you." Joseph knew and testified that God alone could give the meanings of these dreams.

The Butler's Dream Explained:

Ge 40:9-13 "And the chief butler told his dream to Joseph, and said to him, In my dream, behold, a vine *was* before me; And in the vine *were* three branches: and it *was* as though it budded, *and* her blossoms shot forth; and the clusters thereof brought forth ripe grapes: And Pharaoh's cup *was* in my hand: and I took the grapes, and pressed them into Pharaoh's cup, and I gave the cup into Pharaoh's hand. And Joseph said unto him, This *is* the interpretation of it: The three branches *are* three days: Yet within three days shall Pharaoh lift up thine head, and restore thee unto thy place: and thou shalt deliver Pharaoh's cup into his hand, after the former manner when thou wast his butler. "

God showed Joseph the meaning of the butler's dream instantly. For the butler, the interpretation was the best possible news. In three days, Pharaoh would free him from prison and restore him back to his position as chief butler. To him, this must have seemed too good to be true. But God's Word is always sure. We can learn some things from the interpretation of the butler's dream. First of all, God rewarded the faith of Joseph. Joseph's faith was in God alone to give the answer to this dream, and God blessed Joseph with immediate understanding. We also see that God knows the end from the beginning. God is the eternal God, and He knows the future down to the smallest detail. This is shown in the detailed interpretation of the butler's dream. God gave the exact time when it would come to pass- three days. It's hard to imagine that the butler would go from prison right back into the king's service in that short length of time, but God would do it. We learn from this that God's Word is clear and specific. It is not full of confusion and foolishness. In our day, even as in Joseph's time, there are those who claim to be prophets and soothsayers who try to predict things that will happen by their own foolishness or by Satan's power. Their predictions are vague and unspecific because they really don't know what's going to happen. Sadly, people follow them. We, like Joseph, have the sure Word of God, and His Word will never fail.

The interpretation of the chief butler's dream by the Lord also shows us something else about the butler. Whatever had happened to offend Pharaoh was something that the butler was not guilty of. God knows the innocent from the guilty, and in mercy, He showed this man that He would restore him to his former position and save his life. Later, we will see that God had another reason for sparing the chief butler's life that would fulfill His purpose for Joseph.

<u>Joseph's Request:</u>

Joseph had been a great blessing to this man. He had given the butler the sure word of God concerning his dream, and it was good news. Joseph knew God would bring it to pass, so in faith, he made a particular request of the butler:

Ge 40:13-15 "But think on me when it shall be well with thee, and shew kindness, I pray thee, unto me, and make mention of me unto Pharaoh, and bring me out of this house: For indeed I was stolen away out of the land of the Hebrews: and here also have I done nothing that they should put me into the dungeon."

Joseph's request to the chief butler is the first record we have of him talking to anyone about what had happened to him. No doubt he had cried out to the Lord for help many times through the long years. But the request he made of the butler showed his faith in the fact that God would fulfill His word and restore this man to his position of influence in the court of the king. Joseph humbly asked the butler to think of him and make mention of him to Pharaoh when God restored him to his position. Joseph had suffered great wrong at the hands of his brothers; yet even when he spoke of his suffering to the butler at this time, he did not tell him what his brothers had done to him or about anyone else who had wronged him. He only proclaimed the truth concerning his own life- that he had been wrongfully stolen from his home and land, and that he had done nothing to merit being imprisoned in the dungeon. He was innocent of the accusations that had put him there. Joseph pled for kindness and mercy from a man whom he knew God had placed in his life.

Joseph's response to his suffering is such a good example to us of how we should respond when others wrong us. At such times, we are often tempted to get back at those who have hurt us, to wrong them in return or to speak evil of them; but Joseph entrusted himself and his brothers to God. He did not allow bitterness toward man to harden his heart. In this he was so much like our Lord Jesus. Remember that Jesus, even on the cross, said, "Father, forgive them for they know not what they do." Joseph humbly confessed his innocence, but he did not speak bitterly against those who had wronged him. He did as the Bible tells us we are to do:

1Pe 2:21-23 "For even hereunto were ye called: because Christ also suffered for us, leaving us an example, that ye should follow his steps: Who did no sin, neither was guile found in his mouth: Who, when he was reviled, reviled not again; when he suffered, he threatened not; but committed *himself* to him that judgeth righteously."

Joseph committed himself to the Lord "that judgeth righteously." He knew that God alone could make things right for him and hoped that perhaps God would use this man to help him.

The Baker's Dream:

Ge 40:16-19 "When the chief baker saw that the interpretation was good, he said unto Joseph, I also *was* in my dream, and, behold, *I had* three white baskets on my head: And in the uppermost basket *there was* of all manner of bakemeats for Pharaoh; and the birds did eat them out of the basket upon my head. And Joseph answered and said, This *is* the interpretation thereof: The three baskets *are* three days: Yet within three days shall Pharaoh lift up thy head from off thee, and shall hang thee on a tree; and the birds shall eat thy flesh from off thee."

When the baker heard the favorable interpretation of the butler's dream, he was eager to hear how his dream would turn out. He apparently didn't consider that the interpretation of his dream would be the true and just judgment of God upon him, just as it had been upon his innocent companion. Joseph did not mince any words with the baker. He gave him God's sure word concerning his future, just as he had the butler's. In three days, the baker would be executed for his crime and his body hung upon a tree for the birds to eat. It was not a pretty picture, but it was the truth, and reflected the perfection of God's justice. God's judgment is always right. The baker may have thought that he would get away with whatever he had done, but God had seen it. God gave His righteous verdict on the baker through his dream. God is merciful to sinners who turn from their sin in repentance, but God has a deadline for all who persist in wickedness and who try to cover their sin. We read of God's righteous judgment in Exodus 34 and Ezekiel 18:

Ex. 34:6-7" ...The LORD, The LORD God, merciful and gracious, longsuffering, and abundant in goodness and truth, Keeping mercy for thousands, forgiving iniquity and transgression and sin, and that will by no means clear *the guilty...*"

Eze 18:20 "The soul that sinneth, it shall die."

Joseph told the baker God's plain truth. We live in a time when people don't like to hear God's plain truth concerning sin; but God's Word is still true. It will not fail. When we tell people about Jesus Christ, we have to give them the good news and the bad news. The good news is that God has provided forgiveness, salvation, and an eternal home in Heaven through His Son, the Lord Jesus Christ. The bad news is that all people are guilty sinners on their way to eternal judgment unless they trust the saving power found in Jesus Christ alone. In the Gospel, the good news takes away all the bad news for those who will receive it. For those who won't turn to Christ, however, the end will be tragic. There is no good news for those who die without Christ. Joseph had no good news for the baker. His sin had caught up with him and would lead to his death.

The Sure Fulfillment of God's Word through Joseph:

Genesis 40:20-22 "And it came to pass the third day, *which was* Pharaoh's birthday, that he made a feast unto all his servants: and he lifted up the head of the chief butler and of the chief baker among his servants. And he restored the chief butler unto his butlership again; and he gave the cup into Pharaoh's hand: But he hanged the chief baker: as Joseph had interpreted to them."

God's word was perfectly fulfilled just as it had been shown to Joseph. In three days, on Pharaoh's birthday, the chief butler was restored to his place of service at the hand of Pharaoh; but the chief baker was hanged- executed for his crimes, as God said he would be.

Unfortunately, though Joseph had been a great help to the chief butler, he forgot to show kindness to the man who had done so much for him:

Genesis 40:23 "Yet did not the chief butler remember Joseph, but forgat him."

Two more weary years of waiting would pass for Joseph in prison. Even though man had forgotten Joseph, God had not forgotten him. Joseph was His loved and precious servant. He could never forget him. It was God's power that would bring Joseph out of prison at God's perfect time. Joseph didn't know the reason then, but one day, he would understand God's timing and His plan. God loves and remembers His children who are suffering for His sake. Maybe you find yourself wondering why God has not answered your prayers concerning something you really desire or need. Don't stop praying. God has His perfect time. He will hear and answer prayer in His way and in His time.

Remember our memory verse:

Ps 37:4-5 "Delight thyself also in the LORD; and he shall give thee the desires of thine heart. Commit thy way unto the LORD; trust also in him; and he shall bring *it* to pass."

In this same Psalm the Lord reminds us:

Ps 37:7-9 "Rest in the LORD, and wait patiently for him: fret not thyself because of him who prospereth in his way, because of the man who bringeth wicked devices to pass. Cease from anger, and forsake wrath: fret not thyself in any wise to do evil. For evildoers shall be cut off: but those that wait upon the LORD, they shall inherit the earth."

No matter our circumstances, we can rest in the Lord and trust Him to make things right as we obey His Word. His presence will be our comfort and stay even in the darkest of circumstances:

"Abide With Me"

Abide with me; fast falls the eventide;
The darkness deepens; Lord, with me abide;
When other helpers fail and comforts flee,
Help of the helpless, oh, abide with me.

Swift to its close ebbs out life's little day;
Earth's joys grow dim, its glories pass away;
Change and decay in all around I see—
O Thou who changest not, abide with me.

I need Thy presence every passing hour;
What but Thy grace can foil the tempter's pow'r?
Who, like Thyself, my guide and stay can be?
Through cloud and sunshine, Lord, abide with me.

I fear no foe, with Thee at hand to bless;
Ills have no weight, and tears no bitterness;
Where is death's sting? Where, grave, thy victory?
I triumph still, if Thou abide with me.

Hold Thou Thy cross before my closing eyes;
Shine through the gloom and point me to the skies;
Heav'n's morning breaks, and earth's vain shadows flee;
In life, in death, O Lord, abide with me.

-Henry F. Lyte, 1847

Chapter 11: "The Life of Joseph" (Part 6)

Memory verses:

Ps 37:5-6 "Commit thy way unto the LORD; trust also in him; and he shall bring *it* to pass. And he shall bring forth thy righteousness as the light, and thy judgment as the noonday."

Scripture Reading: Genesis 41

Key Lessons: God keeps His promises

<u>The Dreams of Pharaoh:</u>

Two full years passed after Joseph's interpretation of the butler and baker's dreams. Though man had forgotten Joseph, God had not forgotten him. He began to move upon the heart of Pharaoh himself:

Ge 41:1-7 "And it came to pass at the end of two full years, that Pharaoh dreamed: and, behold, he stood by the river. And, behold, there came up out of the river seven well favoured kine and fatfleshed; and they fed in a meadow. And, behold, seven other kine came up after them out of the river, ill favoured and leanfleshed; and stood by the *other* kine upon the brink of the river. And the ill favoured and leanfleshed kine did eat up the seven well favoured and fat kine. So Pharaoh awoke. And he slept and dreamed the second time: and, behold, seven ears of corn came up upon one stalk, rank and good. And, behold, seven thin ears and blasted with the east wind sprung up after them. And the seven thin ears devoured the seven rank and full ears. And Pharaoh awoke, and, behold, *it was* a dream."

This time, God spoke through dreams to Pharaoh, the king of Egypt. The river in Pharaoh's dream was the Nile River which runs through Egypt to this day. Ancient Egypt was built along the banks of the Nile for a reason. In fact, the Nile River was the very source of Egypt's survival. *The American Tract Society Dictionary* notes the following:

"As rain very seldom falls, even in winter, in Southern Egypt, and usually only slight and infrequent showers in Lower Egypt, the whole physical and political existence of Egypt may be said to depend on the Nile; since without this river, and even without its regular annual inundation's, the whole land would be but a desert."

Though Egypt is located in the middle of a desert, the Nile River overflows its banks every year and deposits rich mud called silt over all the surrounding land. As a result, Egypt is a very fertile country even in the midst of a barren wilderness. The setting of Pharaoh's first dream was upon the banks of this most important natural resource Egypt had.

In his dream, Pharaoh stood on the bank of the Nile. Since the Egyptians viewed the Nile as sacred, the setting of this dream carried supernatural significance for Pharaoh. Pharaoh himself was worshipped and considered divine by the Egyptians. They worshipped many false gods, including a god of the river. Pharaoh didn't understand that the true God- the God of Heaven -created all these things. The cows in Pharaoh's dream came up out of the Nile River. Seven of them were fat and beautiful. They came up out of the river where they fed peacefully in a meadow. What a beautiful picture! But how shocking it was when seven skinny and sickly cows came up out of the river and ate up the fat, beautiful cows!

Have you ever had a dream that woke you because it was so shocking and real? This is how Pharaoh must have felt after his dream. Cows don't eat other cows. This was a bizarre and hideous dream! What could it mean? Pharaoh fell asleep again and dreamed a second dream. This time his dream was about a vital food crop- corn.

Corn is a staple food in many countries, like rice, wheat, or potatoes. Staple crops provide the basis for a country's diet. When such crops die because of lack of rain, or disease, or insects, it causes a shortage of food in the whole country and brings starvation. You may have heard of the potato famine in Ireland in the 1800's. That famine came because of a disease that destroyed the potato crop in Ireland for several years in a row. Potatoes were the basis of Ireland's food supply at that time. Because the potato crops were destroyed, people literally starved to death (*Encyclopedia Britannica*, "Great Famine, Ireland").

Corn was the staple crop of Egypt in Joseph's day. It was vital not only for the Egyptians but for the entire world of that time. It was an evil omen indeed when the good, fat ears of corn were devoured by the thin, poor ones. Once again Pharaoh awoke. It had all been a dream.

Ge 41:8-13 "And it came to pass in the morning that his spirit was troubled; and he sent and called for all the magicians of Egypt, and all the wise men thereof: and Pharaoh told them his dream; but *there was* none that could interpret them unto Pharaoh. Then spake the chief butler unto Pharaoh, saying, I do remember my faults this day: Pharaoh was wroth with his servants, and put me in ward in the captain of the guard's house, *both* me and the chief baker: And we dreamed a dream in one night, I and he; we dreamed each man according to the interpretation of his dream. And *there was* there with us a young man, an Hebrew, servant to the captain of the guard; and we told him, and he interpreted to us our dreams; to each man according to his dream he did interpret. And it came to pass, as he interpreted to us, so it was; me he restored unto mine office, and him he hanged."

The Helplessness of Pharaoh's Servants to Discern Spiritual Truth:

Once again we see that Pharaoh knew that these were not ordinary dreams. There was a supernatural message behind them, and he had to find out what it was. He sent for all of his magicians and wise men to help, but when he told them his dreams, they couldn't decipher them. Since they didn't know the living God, they couldn't understand the truth of God behind Pharaoh's dreams. There is a principle we can learn in this today. The Bible says:

1Co 2:14-15 "But the natural man receiveth not the things of the Spirit of God: for they are foolishness unto him: neither can he know *them*, because they are spiritually discerned. But he that is spiritual judgeth all things..."

This Scripture tells us that an unsaved person does not understand the things of God. He cannot understand them, because God's truth is spiritually discerned- it can only be understood through the Spirit of God. Since the Christian has the Spirit of God living within, he can understand God's truth. God's Spirit reveals His truth to us as we seek it in God's Word and depend upon Him to guide us. To the lost, the things of God seem foolish. This is why the lost may persecute and ridicule the saved and think that the way we live is foolish. They don't understand the truth or goodness of God until they turn to Him for salvation themselves. The lost live as they do because, until they are saved, they are cut off from the light of God. The Bible says that Satan, the god of this world, has blinded the minds of those who do not believe. Their understanding is darkened by the devil because of their unbelief (2 Co. 4:4). This is one of the many reasons we must share the gospel with others- so that they too can have the light of God shining in their hearts and understand God's truth.

The Chief Butler Finally Speaks:

When Pharaoh turned to these magicians and wise men for help, they couldn't help him at all. The truth of God revealed in Pharaoh's dreams made no sense to them. But God was going to bring forth his man to tell God's truth to them. This was God's perfect time. Pharaoh was now ready to listen. Finally, after two long years, the chief butler remembered Joseph's request to show kindness to him. He told the king how Joseph had interpreted both his and the chief baker's dreams perfectly. All had come to pass just as Joseph had told them. The chief butler called Joseph "a Hebrew." The word "Hebrew" was first used in Genesis 14:13 where Abraham is called "Abram the Hebrew." Joseph said he had been "stolen out of the land of the Hebrews." Potiphar's wife had also disparagingly called Joseph "an Hebrew." The Hebrews were the descendants of Abraham, Isaac, and Joseph's father, Israel. Already, God was beginning to fulfill His promise to Abraham to make of him a great nation. In just a short period of time, the descendants of Abraham were already known as "Hebrews"- the people of the living God.

When Pharaoh heard about Joseph, he sent for him immediately:

Ge 41:14-16 "Then Pharaoh sent and called Joseph, and they brought him hastily out of the dungeon: and he shaved *himself*, and changed his raiment, and came in unto Pharaoh. And Pharaoh said unto Joseph, I have dreamed a dream, and *there is* none that can interpret it: and I have heard say of thee, *that* thou canst understand a dream to interpret it. And Joseph answered Pharaoh, saying, *It is* not in me: God shall give Pharaoh an answer of peace."

Joseph's Godly Testimony Shown in his Preparation:

God was working in a wondrous way to fulfill His promises to Joseph. Pharaoh's servants brought Joseph out of the prison, called in verse 14, "the dungeon." The word "dungeon" gives us an idea of the awful darkness of the place where Joseph had been locked up all these years. According to *Webster's 1828 Dictionary*, a dungeon is "a deep, dark place of confinement." It was a horrible and depressing place. How wonderful it must have been for Joseph to be brought out of this gloomy place, and, incredibly, he was being brought out to stand before Pharaoh himself.

Before he went before the king, the Bible says that Joseph shaved himself and changed his raiment. Joseph was respectful to authority. He wanted to be a good testimony to the king. We can learn something else about Joseph from this. How we dress and present ourselves to others affects our testimony for the Lord. When we come to church we ought to dress in a way that shows reverence to the Lord and respect for God's people. How we dress from day to day shows our reverence for God and His Word as well. You may say, "But does it really matter how I dress? After all, doesn't the Bible say, 'Man looketh on the outward appearance, but God looketh upon the heart'" (1 Sa. 16:7)? Indeed, the Bible does say that, but the verse that says that is not talking about clothing, but about physical characteristics- things that are part of our innate physical makeup. In 1 Samuel 16, God was warning Samuel not to be impressed with the outward appearance of the candidates for Israel's king; for God would choose a king based upon the heart, not a handsome face or impressive physique. We cannot take a verse out of the context of Scripture and use it however we like. God gives the interpretation of His Word plainly to those who seek His wisdom. God alone sees the heart, but He does see the outside as well, and God has given very clear guidelines in His Word concerning how His holy people should dress.

1Timothy 2:9-10 specifically tells us that Christian women should dress in modest apparel- clothes that cover properly and are not sensual and alluring in character. Our clothing is to be a reflection of a godly character. And, since man can only see the outward appearance, how we dress does affect our testimony to others. Our clothing should reflect a submissive and holy heart toward God. For Christian women, our clothing should be distinctly feminine and modest. Christian men should also dress in a way that is modest and masculine. When we dress to go out, we should think, "Would God be pleased with what I'm wearing?" "Is it modest?" "Does my clothing and appearance reflect the fact that I belong to God?" When we see a woman in a modest skirt or dress, we automatically think she may be a Christian because she is dressing according to godliness. This pleases the Lord and presents a good testimony. Modesty and gender-specific clothing are clear Biblical principles God has given in His Word. Sadly, dressing for the Lord is not very popular in our culture today, but God's Word has not changed. We are to be reverent and respectful to God and to present a good testimony, even in the way we dress. Joseph was careful to present a good testimony when he came before Pharaoh.

Joseph Gives Glory to God:

When Joseph appeared before Pharaoh, we see again how eager Joseph was to give glory to God alone. He did not take the opportunity to present his own case to Pharaoh. He knew he could trust God to take care of him. He came ready to serve and to help others. Pharaoh told Joseph his problem- no one could interpret his dreams. He had been told that Joseph could understand and interpret them. Joseph's answer showed his humility and his dependence upon the Lord alone when he said:

"... *It is* not in me: God shall give Pharaoh an answer of peace."

Joseph was a great example to us of humility. He did not take credit for anything. He gave glory to God and freely confessed that he did not have the ability to interpret these dreams. God alone could do that. The Bible tells us that "...God resisteth the proud, but giveth grace to the humble" (James 4:6). Joseph had learned the blessing of humbling himself before God.
1Pe 5:6-7 "Humble yourselves therefore under the mighty hand of God, that he may exalt you in due time: Casting all your care upon him; for he careth for you."

Throughout his life, Joseph had humbled himself before God and trusted Him to keep His promises to him. Now, as he stood before the king, he testified to Pharaoh of the wisdom of God. Also, with compassion for the anxiety of the king concerning these dreams, he reassured the king that God would give Pharaoh "an answer of peace."

Pharaoh's Dream and God's Answer:

Ge 41:17-32 "And Pharaoh said unto Joseph, In my dream, behold, I stood upon the bank of the river: And, behold, there came up out of the river seven kine, fatfleshed and well favoured; and they fed in a meadow: And, behold, seven other kine came up after them, poor and very ill favoured and leanfleshed, such as I never saw in all the land of Egypt for badness: And the lean and the ill favoured kine did eat up the first seven fat kine: And when they had eaten them up, it could not be known that they had eaten them; but they *were* still ill favoured, as at the beginning. So I awoke. And I saw in my dream, and, behold, seven ears came up in one stalk, full and good: And, behold, seven ears, withered, thin, *and* blasted with the east wind, sprung up after them: And the thin ears devoured the seven good ears: and I told *this* unto the magicians; but *there was* none that could declare *it* to me. And Joseph said unto Pharaoh, The dream of Pharaoh *is* one: God hath shewed Pharaoh what he *is* about to do. The seven good kine *are* seven years; and the seven good ears *are* seven years: the dream *is* one. And the seven thin and ill favoured kine that came up after them *are* seven years; and the seven empty ears blasted with the east wind shall be seven years of famine. This *is* the thing which I have spoken unto Pharaoh: What God *is* about to do he sheweth unto Pharaoh. Behold, there come seven years of great plenty throughout all the land of Egypt: And there shall arise after them seven years of famine; and all the plenty shall be forgotten in the land of Egypt; and the famine shall consume the land; And the plenty shall not be known in the land by reason of that famine following; for it *shall be* very grievous. And for that the dream was doubled unto Pharaoh twice; *it is* because the thing *is* established by God, and God will shortly bring it to pass."

Pharaoh recounted his dreams to Joseph. One detail Pharaoh added in his account to Joseph was that when the thin, bad cows ate up the fine, fat cows, the thin cows were unchanged- they were just as thin as before. This had been an especially troubling aspect of the dream, and it had a meaning as well, as God would show Joseph. The dream of the cows and the dream of the corn were one and the same dream as to their meaning. God was graciously showing Pharaoh what He was about to do so that Pharaoh could be prepared for it. God immediately gave Joseph the meaning of the dreams. There would be seven years of wondrous plenty- crops in great abundance -followed by seven years of terrible famine. The years of famine would be so bad that the years of plenty would be forgotten. This was why the thin cows in Pharaoh's dream were unchanged after eating up the fat, good cows. The years of famine would wipe out all that had been gained in the years of plenty. God gave the dream in two forms to Pharaoh, because these things would surely come to pass, and in a very short time. God then gave Joseph wisdom to give Pharaoh some very good advice- advice that would not only save Egypt, but Joseph's own family.

<u>Joseph's Advice and God's Reward:</u>

Ge 41:33-46 "Now therefore let Pharaoh look out a man discreet and wise, and set him over the land of Egypt. Let Pharaoh do *this*, and let him appoint officers over the land, and take up the fifth part of the land of Egypt in the seven plenteous years. And let them gather all the food of those good years that come, and lay up corn under the hand of Pharaoh, and let them keep food in the cities. And that food shall be for store to the land against the seven years of famine, which shall be in the land of Egypt; that the land perish not through the famine. And the thing was good in the eyes of Pharaoh, and in the eyes of all his servants. And Pharaoh said unto his servants, Can we find *such a one* as this *is*, a man in whom the Spirit of God *is*? And Pharaoh said unto Joseph, Forasmuch as God hath shewed thee all this, *there is* none so discreet and wise as thou *art:* Thou shalt be over my house, and according unto thy word shall all my people be ruled: only in the throne will I be greater than thou. And Pharaoh said unto Joseph, See, I have set thee over all the land of Egypt. And Pharaoh took off his ring from his hand, and put it upon Joseph's hand, and arrayed him in vestures of fine linen, and put a gold chain about his neck; And he made him to ride in the second chariot which he had; and they cried before him, Bow the knee: and he made him *ruler* over all the land of Egypt. And Pharaoh said unto Joseph, I *am* Pharaoh, and without thee shall no man lift up his hand or foot in all the land of Egypt. And Pharaoh called Joseph's name Zaphnathpaaneah; and he gave him to wife Asenath the daughter of Potipherah priest of On. And Joseph went out over *all* the land of Egypt. And Joseph *was* thirty years old when he stood before Pharaoh king of Egypt. And Joseph went out from the presence of Pharaoh, and went throughout all the land of Egypt."

What a miracle! In one day, Joseph went from being a prisoner in a dungeon to being the ruler of all Egypt, second only to Pharaoh himself! Only God could do this. After thirteen long years of suffering and obedience, Joseph was exalted to the place God had promised him in his dreams so many years before. When it was God's time to fulfill His word, He did it very quickly. Remember our memory verse:

Ps 37:5 "Commit thy way unto the LORD, trust also in Him and He shall bring it to pass."

God does not fail, and as He promised, He exalts the humble in due time. Though Pharaoh was a pagan man, he knew that Joseph had the Spirit of the living God working through him. There could be no better man to rule Egypt than this humble man of God. God gave Joseph not only an exalted position; he also gave him a wife. God is a faithful and loving God. He gives us more than we ask for, and He gives us His best when we trust and obey Him.

Personal Reflection:

Do you feel like you are waiting a long time for something that you desire and have prayed for? God has a perfect plan and a perfect time. Like Joseph, the LORD wants us to wait for Him and obey His Word. When the time is right, He will answer, and He will bring His perfect will to pass.

"Have Faith in God"

Have faith in God when your pathway is lonely.
He sees and knows all the way you have trod;
Never alone are the least of His children;
Have faith in God, have faith in God.

Have faith in God when your prayers are unanswered,
Your earnest plea He will never forget;
Wait on the Lord, trust His Word and be patient,
Have faith in God. He'll answer yet.

Have faith in God though all else fail about you;
Have faith in God, He provides for His own:
He cannot fail though all kingdoms shall perish.
He rules. He reigns upon His throne.

Have faith in God, He's on His throne,
Have faith in God, He watches o'er His own;
He cannot fail, He must prevail,
Have faith in God, Have faith in God.

-B. B. McKinney, 1934

Chapter 12: "The Life of Joseph" (Part 7)

Memory verses:

Ps 37:4-5 "Delight thyself also in the LORD; and he shall give thee the desires of thine heart. Commit thy way unto the LORD; trust also in him; and he shall bring *it* to pass."

Ro 8:28 "And we know that all things work together for good to them that love God, to them who are the called according to *his* purpose."

Ps 40:1-3 "I waited patiently for the LORD; and he inclined unto me, and heard my cry. He brought me up also out of an horrible pit, out of the miry clay, and set my feet upon a rock, *and* established my goings. And he hath put a new song in my mouth, *even* praise unto our God: many shall see *it*, and fear, and shall trust in the LORD."

Scripture Reading: Genesis 41-42

Key Lessons: God Keeps His Promises; God gives wisdom to those who seek Him

Miraculously, Joseph went from being a prisoner in the king's dungeon to being appointed the governor of the entire land of Egypt- all in one day. What an amazing change in his situation! When Joseph was but a seventeen year old lad, God had shown him that one day he would be placed in a position of great honor; but who could have imagined all the events that would happen before those dreams were fulfilled- and how quickly God would bring it all to pass when the time was right. We read in Genesis 41:46 that "...Joseph was thirty years old when he stood before Pharaoh, king of Egypt." When Pharaoh saw the wisdom of Joseph, he appointed him governor over the whole land to store up food for the years of famine and to prepare the nation for the dark days ahead.

<u>**The Blessed Years of Plenty in Egypt (Genesis 41:47-53):**</u>

Ge 41:47-53 "And in the seven plenteous years the earth brought forth by handfuls. And he gathered up all the food of the seven years, which were in the land of Egypt, and laid up the food in the cities: the food of the field, which *was* round

about every city, laid he up in the same. And Joseph gathered corn as the sand of the sea, very much, until he left numbering; for *it was* without number. And unto Joseph were born two sons before the years of famine came, which Asenath the daughter of Potipherah priest of On bare unto him. And Joseph called the name of the firstborn Manasseh: For God, *said he*, hath made me forget all my toil, and all my father's house. And the name of the second called he Ephraim: For God hath caused me to be fruitful in the land of my affliction. And the seven years of plenteousness, that was in the land of Egypt, were ended."

As we come to Genesis 41:47, the seven years of great blessing and plenty had begun. It says, "And in the seven plenteous years the earth brought forth by handfuls." In verse 49, it says, "And Joseph gathered corn as the sand of the sea, very much, until he left numbering; for it was without number." Can you imagine that? Corn as plentiful as the sand of the sea! We can assume that never in the history of Egypt had there been such an abundant harvest. It was amazing. If God had not shown Pharaoh that seven years of terrible famine were coming after that, the abundant harvest would no doubt have been wasted. God had placed Joseph in this position for a purpose- to save "much people alive" as Genesis 50:20 tells us. Joseph wisely stored up the abundance of grain in the cities of Egypt to prepare for the coming famine (41:48). During those years of plenty, God gave another special blessing to Joseph. He gave Joseph and his wife two sons- Manasseh and Ephraim. Manasseh means "forgetting," for Joseph said, "God hath made me to forget all my toil, and all my father's house." Ephraim means "fruitful," and Joseph said, "God hath caused me to be fruitful in the land of my affliction" (Ge. 41:51-52). God had truly blessed Joseph after all his years of suffering.

The Seven Years of Famine Begin (Genesis 41:54-57):

Ge 41:54-57 "And the seven years of dearth began to come, according as Joseph had said: and the dearth was in all lands; but in all the land of Egypt there was bread. And when all the land of Egypt was famished, the people cried to Pharaoh for bread: and Pharaoh said unto all the Egyptians, Go unto Joseph; what he saith to you, do. And the famine was over all the face of the earth: And Joseph opened all the storehouses, and sold unto the Egyptians; and the famine waxed sore in the land of Egypt. And all countries came into Egypt to Joseph for to buy *corn*; because that the famine was *so* sore in all lands."

We see from these verses that the famine in Joseph's day was not only in Egypt. It was a world-wide dearth. The word "dearth" means extreme hunger- hunger brought about by a lack of natural resources. Many conditions can cause famine- war, insects, and natural disasters -but in most cases, famine is caused by a lack of rain. The land cannot grow crops without sufficient water. Since Egypt's fertility depended on the annual flooding of the Nile rather than rain, famine normally came to Egypt when something blocked the Nile's annual flood cycle (*International Standard Bible Encyclopedia*, "Nile"). Whatever the underlying causes of the famine in Joseph's day, the dearth was sent by God to accomplish His great purpose for His people and for the world as a whole.

Because "the famine was all over the face of the earth," every country throughout the entire world experienced a shortage of food. But since God had raised Joseph up as the governor of Egypt, and he had wisely stored the abundant harvest, there was still food in Egypt. Finally, the famine ravaged Egypt too. The people ran out of their own stores of grain throughout the land, and they cried out to Pharaoh for help. There was only one man whom God had provided to help save the people- Joseph. Pharaoh told them, "Go unto Joseph. What he saith unto you, do." So Joseph opened the storehouses of grain in the cities of Egypt and sold grain to the Egyptians. But because the famine was in all other lands, all the other countries came to Egypt to buy corn from Joseph too.

Joseph, a Picture of Our Savior:

God used Joseph to be a blessing to every country of the world. He became a wonderful picture of God's salvation provided to us in Jesus Christ; for just as the famine affected every part of the world in the days of Joseph, there is an even more terrible famine that affects every person born into the world. It is the famine of the soul caused by sin. Every person born into this world is a sinner separated from the life of God and headed for eternal death. But God sent the Savior- the Lord Jesus Christ -into the world to provide salvation for helpless sinners. Christ is the only hope for the hungry soul. And just as the people of Joseph's day had to come to him for life-saving food or face certain death, so we must come to Christ alone for our salvation to be saved from eternal death. We cannot save ourselves. We must come to Christ. Unlike the food of Joseph's day that had to be bought with money, salvation is a free gift to sinners who will come to Christ for it. We can never pay for it or earn it. We must simply receive it by faith. Though salvation is offered as a free gift to sinners, it was not without cost for Christ. He paid for this great salvation with His own blood when He died on the cross. So we see the wondrous picture here again in the life of Joseph of salvation, not only from the physical death of famine, but salvation from eternal death in hell through Christ. That is why Jesus said:

Joh 6:35 "... I am the bread of life: he that cometh to me shall never hunger; and he that believeth on me shall never thirst."

Any person who is willing to turn from their own way and believe on Christ will receive this wonderful gift of everlasting life:

Joh 3:16 "For God so loved the world, that he gave his only begotten Son, that whosoever believeth in him should not perish, but have everlasting life."

In Genesis 42, we see how God would use Joseph to bring salvation not only to people all over the world who came to him in Egypt, but also to his own family.

Joseph's dream fulfilled concerning his brothers: (Genesis 42-43):

Genesis 42 tells us that Jacob, Joseph's father, heard that there was corn in Egypt. The famine had come to the land of the Hebrews just as it had to the rest of the world. They too, were in danger of starving to death:

Ge 42:1-4 "Now when Jacob saw that there was corn in Egypt, Jacob said unto his sons, Why do ye look one upon another? And he said, Behold, I have heard that there is corn in Egypt: get you down thither, and buy for us from thence; that we may live, and not die. And Joseph's ten brethren went down to buy corn in Egypt. But Benjamin, Joseph's brother, Jacob sent not with his brethren; for he said, Lest peradventure mischief befall him."

Remember, that Jacob had two wives, Rachel and Leah. He had only two sons by his beloved wife, Rachel- Joseph and Benjamin. Rachel had died when Benjamin was born, and, at this time, Jacob (Israel) thought Joseph was dead. He had grieved for his son, Joseph, for thirteen years. Benjamin was all he had left of his wife Rachel- or so he thought. He would not trust his precious Benjamin to leave his sight. He sent his other ten sons to Egypt to buy food for the family. It is interesting to note that all ten of his other sons went on this journey. This was all in the plan of God. Remember, Joseph's dream of the sheaves (Ge. 37)? The dream involved sheaves of grain. All of Joseph's brothers' sheaves had bowed down to Joseph's sheaf. Joseph's brothers coming to him in Egypt to buy grain was a fulfillment of Joseph's first dream in perfect detail- with one exception. His younger brother, Benjamin, was not with them. Through Joseph's dealing with his brothers, God would bring his brother Benjamin to him as well, and would bring together all the details necessary to fulfill Joseph's first and second dreams perfectly.

Ge 42:5-8 "And the sons of Israel came to buy *corn* among those that came: for the famine was in the land of Canaan. And Joseph *was* the governor over the land, *and* he *it was* that sold to all the people of the land: and Joseph's brethren came, and bowed down themselves before him *with* their faces to the earth. And Joseph saw his brethren, and he knew them, but made himself strange unto them, and spake roughly unto them; and he said unto them, Whence come ye? And they said, From the land of Canaan to buy food. And Joseph knew his brethren, but they knew not him. And Joseph remembered the dreams which he dreamed of them, and said unto them, Ye *are* spies; to see the nakedness of the land ye are come."

We can only imagine how Joseph must have felt at this moment. Here were his ten brethren come to buy corn from him as the governor of Egypt, and all of them were bowing down to him with their faces to the earth. He knew that God had fulfilled His word to him. Verse nine tells us that "Joseph remembered the dreams which he dreamed of them..." Joseph recognized his brothers instantly, but they did not recognize their little brother whom they had sold as a slave so many years before. Joseph did not make himself known to them, but instead the Bible says, "He made himself strange unto them, and spake roughly unto them."

Joseph would not reveal himself to them at that time. First, his brethren would have to go through some testing and soul searching of their own hearts. In Genesis 42:13, Joseph's brothers told him:

Ge 42:13-17 "...Thy servants *are* twelve brethren, the sons of one man in the land of Canaan; and, behold, the youngest *is* this day with our father, and one *is* not."

Joseph knew that his younger brother, Benjamin, must also be present for his dream to be completely fulfilled. He accused his brothers of being spies and demanded that they bring their youngest brother before him to prove that they were all sons of one father who had come to Egypt to buy grain:

Ge 42:14-17 "And Joseph said unto them, That *is it* that I spake unto you, saying, Ye *are* spies: Hereby ye shall be proved: By the life of Pharaoh ye shall not go forth hence, except your youngest brother come hither. Send one of you, and let him fetch your brother, and ye shall be kept in prison, that your words may be proved, whether *there be any* truth in you: or else by the life of Pharaoh surely ye *are* spies. And he put them all together into ward three days."

Now, Joseph's brothers were getting a small taste of the suffering they had put their brother Joseph through. They were falsely accused of being spies and put in prison for three days. This was part of God's judging hand upon them to bring them to repentance for all that they had done. Sin always comes back to us in some way. It always has its bitter consequences. As the Bible says in Galatians 6:7, "Be not deceived; God is not mocked: for whatsoever a man soweth, that shall he also reap." Joseph's brothers had spent the last thirteen years living with the guilt of what they had done. They had watched their father grieving over the loss of Joseph because of their deeds and the lies they had concocted to cover their sin. Now their sin was being visited upon them, and they knew it:

Ge 42:18-24 "And Joseph said unto them the third day, This do, and live; *for* I fear God: If ye *be* true *men*, let one of your brethren be bound in the house of your prison: go ye, carry corn for the famine of your houses: But bring your youngest brother unto me; so shall your words be verified, and ye shall not die. And they did so. And they said one to another, We *are* verily guilty concerning our brother, in that we saw the anguish of his soul, when he besought us, and we would not hear; therefore is this distress come upon us. And Reuben answered them, saying, Spake I not unto you, saying, Do not sin against the child; and ye would not hear? therefore, behold, also his blood is required. And they knew not that Joseph understood *them*; for he spake unto them by an interpreter. And he turned himself about from them, and wept; and returned to them again, and communed with them, and took from them Simeon, and bound him before their eyes."

It broke Joseph's heart to hear his brothers talk among themselves as they realized their sins were being visited upon them. He turned from them and wept. It was all coming back to them. They had heard Joseph beg them for mercy. They had seen the anguish of his soul as he was brutally bound and taken as a slave. They had hardened their hearts against his cries for help and let him be taken from his home and his father. Now God's righteous judgment was coming upon them. They watched as their brother Simeon was bound before their eyes. He would be kept a prisoner until they returned with their younger brother to prove their words were true.

Ge 42:25-28 "Then Joseph commanded to fill their sacks with corn, and to restore every man's money into his sack, and to give them provision for the way: and thus did he unto them. And they laded their asses with the corn, and departed thence. And as one of them opened his sack to give his ass provender in the inn, he espied his money; for, behold, it *was* in his sack's mouth. And he said unto his brethren, My money is restored; and, lo, *it is* even in my sack: and their heart failed *them*, and they were afraid, saying one to another, What *is* this *that* God hath done unto us?"

Joseph took care of his family, even though they did not know who he was. He made sure they had corn to take back to his father and to their families. He not only gave them the grain they needed, but provisions for their journey, and he restored every man's money back into his sack of grain. This he did not only to bless them- for all that he gave them was a gift of grace -but also to test them. When one of the brothers found that his money had been restored, all the brothers were terrified. They did not understand why the man who treated them so roughly would return their money to them. They could only assume one thing- this too was part of God's judgment upon them. They feared they were being set up and would be accused as thieves and condemned to prison. The noose was tightening around their necks, and it was all because of what they had done to their brother, Joseph, so many years before.

Ge 42:29-35 "And they came unto Jacob their father unto the land of Canaan, and told him all that befell unto them; saying, The man, *who is* the lord of the land, spake roughly to us, and took us for spies of the country. And we said unto him, We *are* true *men*; we are no spies: We *be* twelve brethren, sons of our father; one *is* not, and the youngest *is* this day with our father in the land of Canaan. And the man, the lord of the country, said unto us, Hereby shall I know that ye *are* true *men*; leave one of your brethren *here* with me, and take *food for* the famine of your households, and be gone: And bring your youngest brother unto me: then shall I know that ye *are* no spies, but *that* ye *are* true *men: so* will I deliver you your brother, and ye shall traffick in the land. And it came to pass as they emptied their sacks, that, behold, every man's bundle of money *was* in his sack: and when *both* they and their father saw the bundles of money, they were afraid."

When they returned home, they explained to their father Jacob all that had happened to them in Egypt- how the man in charge had demanded that they bring Benjamin back with them to prove they were not spies and how he had kept Simeon prisoner. Then, when they began to empty their sacks of grain, they discovered that every man's bundle of money had been returned to him in his sack! Both they and their father were afraid of what this might mean and what would become of them. But Jacob would not consider allowing Benjamin to go back with them. Even with Simeon kept as prisoner and with all of Reuben's passionate pleading, he would not entrust his last and dearest son to them. Jacob said,

Ge 42:36-38 "And Jacob their father said unto them, Me have ye bereaved *of my children*: Joseph *is* not, and Simeon *is* not, and ye will take Benjamin *away*: all these things are against me. And Reuben spake unto his father, saying, Slay my two sons, if I bring him not to thee: deliver him into my hand, and I will bring him to thee again. And he said, My son shall not go down with you; for his brother is dead, and he is left alone: if mischief befall him by the way in the which ye go, then shall ye bring down my gray hairs with sorrow to the grave."

Reuben made his father a foolish offer- to slay his two sons if he didn't bring Benjamin back -as if more death would give any comfort to anyone. This was not godly thinking at all. It is a common way of thinking in our own culture. Children, especially the unborn, are seen as expendable- just garbage to be cast aside as an inconvenience. But God does not view innocent life that way. In fact, the shedding of innocent blood is something that Almighty God hates and will bring to judgment:

Pr 6:16-17 "These six *things* doth the LORD hate: yea, seven *are* an abomination unto him: A proud look, a lying tongue, and hands that shed innocent blood..."
The shedding of innocent blood was one of the main reasons God caused Israel and Judah to be conquered by their enemies and taken as slaves to foreign lands. They had defiled the land with innocent blood. Their idolatrous worship included the offering of innocent babies to their gods. They burned their own children alive as human sacrifices to pagan idols. God's righteous judgment came upon them. The northern kingdom of Israel with its ten tribes was taken by the king of Assyria to his land, and from there, they were scattered to the ends of the earth. They remain scattered throughout the world to this day. The southern kingdom of Judah was taken captive to Babylon where they remained for seventy years:

Ps 106:37-41 "Yea, they sacrificed their sons and their daughters unto devils, And shed innocent blood, *even* the blood of their sons and of their daughters, whom they sacrificed unto the idols of Canaan: and the land was polluted with blood. Thus were they defiled with their own works, and went a whoring with their own inventions. Therefore was the wrath of the LORD kindled against his people, insomuch that he abhorred his own inheritance. And he gave them into the hand of the heathen; and they that hated them ruled over them."

All human life is precious to God. Innocent blood pollutes a land and a nation. God is the Great Creator and Savior of mankind. He gave His own Son to redeem lost sinners of every race. Each person is a creation of His own hand. From conception, human life is precious in the sight of God. The psalmist David wrote of this wondrous miracle in Psalm 139:

Ps 139:13 "For thou hast possessed my reins: thou hast covered me in my mother's womb. I will praise thee; for I am fearfully *and* wonderfully made: marvellous *are* thy works; and *that* my soul knoweth right well. My substance was not hid from thee, when I was made in secret, *and* curiously wrought in the lowest parts of the earth. Thine eyes did see my substance, yet being unperfect; and in thy book all *my members* were written, *which* in continuance were fashioned, when *as yet there was* none of them. How precious also are thy thoughts unto me, O God! how great is the sum of them!"

Every Christian should stand where God stands on the issue of innocent human life. God is the Protector and Defender of the helpless, and He will not hold people guiltless who take part in the shedding of innocent blood. For those who repent, there is still mercy and forgiveness with God, but for those who do not, there is a great judgment day coming:

Re 21:8 "But the fearful, and unbelieving, and the abominable, and murderers, and whoremongers, and sorcerers, and idolaters, and all liars, shall have their part in the lake which burneth with fire and brimstone: which is the second death."

Heb 13:4 "Marriage *is* honourable in all, and the bed undefiled: but whoremongers and adulterers God will judge."

Re 20:12-14 "And I saw the dead, small and great, stand before God; and the books were opened: and another book was opened, which is *the book* of life: and the dead were judged out of those things which were written in the books, according to

Be An Example

their works. And the sea gave up the dead which were in it; and death and hell delivered up the dead which were in them: and they were judged every man according to their works. And death and hell were cast into the lake of fire. This is the second death."

Killing the innocent has never made things better for anyone. In the case of Joseph's brethren, Reuben's godless argument got nowhere with his father. But inevitably, Jacob would have to trust God with Benjamin. When Jacob finally let Benjamin go, God would fulfill His wonderful plan for Israel and his sons. When we are willing to trust God with things that are precious to us, then God can do His perfect work in our lives. His way is always perfect; but to enjoy God's perfect way, we must surrender all to Him- even when we can't see the way ahead or how things can possibly work out for our good. God always does what is right. We can trust in Him.

"Like a River Glorious"

Like a river glorious is God's perfect peace,
Over all victorious, in its bright increase;
Perfect, yet it floweth fuller every day,
Perfect, yet it groweth deeper all the way.

Refrain:
Stayed upon Jehovah, hearts are fully blest
Finding, as He promised, perfect peace and rest.

Hidden in the hollow of His blessed hand,
Never foe can follow, never traitor stand;
Not a surge of worry, not a shade of care,
Not a blast of hurry touch the spirit there.

Every joy or trial falleth from above,
Traced upon our dial by the Sun of Love;
We may trust Him fully, all for us to do;
They who trust Him wholly find Him wholly true.

-Frances R. Havergal, 1876

Chapter 13: "The Life of Joseph" (Part 8)

Memory verses:

Ge 50:19-20   "And Joseph said unto them, Fear not: for *am* I in the place of God? But as for you, ye thought evil against me; *but* God meant it unto good, to bring to pass, as *it is* this day, to save much people alive."

Eph 4:32 "And be ye kind one to another, tenderhearted, forgiving one another, even as God for Christ's sake hath forgiven you."

Col 3:12-14   "Put on therefore, as the elect of God, holy and beloved, bowels of mercies, kindness, humbleness of mind, meekness, longsuffering; Forbearing one another, and forgiving one another, if any man have a quarrel against any: even as Christ forgave you, so also *do ye*. And above all these things *put on* charity, which is the bond of perfectness."

Scripture Reading: Genesis 43-45

Key Lessons: God Keeps His Promises; The Power of Forgiveness

The Return to Egypt:

We learned how God began to fulfill Joseph's first dream of the sheaves. Those sheaves represented Joseph's brothers- all eleven of them -bowing down to Joseph, the governor of all Egypt. God had exalted Joseph to this place. Joseph had been put in charge over all the food during the seven years of great abundance. The Bible says that the corn of Egypt during those years was as the sand of the sea. Joseph had wisely stored the food in all the cities of Egypt in preparation for the seven years of famine to come. When the famine did come, it was dreadful, and the Bible says it was over the face of the whole earth. Only in Egypt was food to be found, so people came from all over the world to buy grain there. Jacob sent his sons to buy food for them as well. All of Israel's sons came except for Benjamin, Joseph's younger brother. Joseph did not reveal himself to his brothers, and they did not recognize him. He accused them of being spies to test them. When Joseph sent his brothers back home, he demanded they bring Benjamin back to stand before him to prove they were not spies. He held Simeon in Egypt as surety of their return.

Joseph knew his dream would not be completely fulfilled until Benjamin came. God was also working to bring Joseph's brothers to repentance for what they had done. When they returned home, the brothers told their father all that had happened to them in Egypt and that they must return with Benjamin if Simeon was to be released. At that time, Jacob would not allow Benjamin to return with them. He was afraid something would happen to Benjamin as it had happened to Joseph. We can certainly understand Jacob's fear. Benjamin was so precious to him, and he had already lost his beloved son, Joseph- or so he thought. He clung to the last precious son of his beloved wife, Rachel. But God wanted Jacob to trust Him even in this.

Jacob would have to let Benjamin go for God's purpose to be accomplished in his life and in the lives of his family. We too must surrender all to the Lord if we would know His perfect will, even when we can't see how things will turn out. We must rest upon the unfailing promises of God. He will not fail or forsake those who trust in Him:

Ps 18:30 "As *for* God, his way *is* perfect: the word of the LORD is tried: he *is* a buckler to all those that trust in him."

Pr 3:5-6 "Trust in the LORD with all thine heart; and lean not unto thine own understanding. In all thy ways acknowledge him, and he shall direct thy paths."

Isa 50:10 "Who *is* among you that feareth the LORD, that obeyeth the voice of his servant, that walketh *in* darkness, and hath no light? let him trust in the name of the LORD, and stay upon his God."

Jacob had to surrender all of his children- even Benjamin -to the Lord. It was not until the grain they had brought back from Egypt was completely gone- when there was no other way -that Jacob finally consented to allow Benjamin to go to Egypt with his brothers.

Ge 43:1-15 "And the famine *was* sore in the land. And it came to pass, when they had eaten up the corn which they had brought out of Egypt, their father said unto them, Go again, buy us a little food. And Judah spake unto him, saying, The man did solemnly protest unto us, saying, Ye shall not see my face, except your brother *be* with you. If thou wilt send our brother with us, we will go down and buy thee food: But if thou wilt not send *him*, we will not go down: for the man said unto us, Ye shall not see my face, except your brother *be* with you. And

Israel said, Wherefore dealt ye *so* ill with me, *as* to tell the man whether ye had yet a brother? And they said, The man asked us straitly of our state, and of our kindred, saying, *Is* your father yet alive? have ye *another* brother? and we told him according to the tenor of these words: could we certainly know that he would say, Bring your brother down? And Judah said unto Israel his father, Send the lad with me, and we will arise and go; that we may live, and not die, both we, and thou, *and* also our little ones. I will be surety for him; of my hand shalt thou require him: if I bring him not unto thee, and set him before thee, then let me bear the blame for ever: For except we had lingered, surely now we had returned this second time. And their father Israel said unto them, If *it must be* so now, do this; take of the best fruits in the land in your vessels, and carry down the man a present, a little balm, and a little honey, spices, and myrrh, nuts, and almonds: And take double money in your hand; and the money that was brought again in the mouth of your sacks, carry *it* again in your hand; peradventure it *was* an oversight: Take also your brother, and arise, go again unto the man: And God Almighty give you mercy before the man, that he may send away your other brother, and Benjamin. If I be bereaved *of my children*, I am bereaved. And the men took that present, and they took double money in their hand, and Benjamin; and rose up, and went down to Egypt, and stood before Joseph."

Judah, Jacob's son who had suggested that Joseph be sold as a slave so many years before (Ge. 37:26-27), now offered himself to his father as surety for the safety of his younger brother, Benjamin. Finally, Jacob surrendered to God's plan.

When they arrived back in Egypt, Joseph saw that they had finally brought Benjamin with them. He told the ruler of his house to bring all of his brothers to his home and prepare a meal for them. The brothers didn't know what was going to happen when they were taken to this ruler's home. They were terrified:

Ge 43:16-23 "And when Joseph saw Benjamin with them, he said to the ruler of his house, Bring *these* men home, and slay, and make ready; for *these* men shall dine with me at noon. And the man did as Joseph bade; and the man brought the men into Joseph's house. And the men were afraid, because they were brought into Joseph's house; and they said, Because of the money that was returned in our sacks at the first time are we brought in; that he may seek occasion against us, and fall upon us, and take us for bondmen, and our asses. And they came near to the steward of Joseph's house, and they communed with him at the door of the house, And said, O sir, we came indeed down at the first time to buy food: And it came to pass, when we came to the inn, that we opened our sacks, and, behold, *every* man's money *was* in the mouth of his sack, our money in full weight: and we have brought it again in our hand. And other money have we brought down in our hands to buy food: we cannot tell who put our money in our sacks. And he said, Peace *be* to you, fear not: your God, and the God of your father, hath given you treasure in your sacks: I had your money. And he brought Simeon out unto them."

Joseph's brothers were experiencing some of the fear they had put Joseph through when they sold him into slavery. They had no idea what was going to happen to them. They feared everything and everyone. They spoke to Joseph's steward- the man in charge of Joseph's household -about the money put back into their sacks. The man reassured them and brought their brother, Simeon, out to them. They would soon receive the shock of their lives- and experience the wondrous grace of God through their brother, Joseph. But first, more testing would come:

Ge 43:24-28 "And the man brought the men into Joseph's house, and gave *them* water, and they washed their feet; and he gave their asses provender. And they made ready the present against Joseph came at noon: for they heard that they should eat bread there. And when Joseph came home, they brought him the present which *was* in their hand into the house, and bowed themselves to him to the earth. And he asked them of *their* welfare, and said, *Is* your father well, the old man of whom ye spake? *Is* he yet alive? And they answered, Thy servant our father *is* in good health, he *is* yet alive. And they bowed down their heads, and made obeisance."

Joseph was a man of great authority and power. He could have used his power to punish his brothers for all that they had done to him. But Joseph was an example to us of God's mercy and forgiveness to undeserving sinners. God too has the power to punish sinners, but He shows them mercy. He seeks to bring men to repentance that He might forgive and save them. He gives food and comfort and love to mankind- even those who reject Him and His Word. Mercy is withholding punishment that is deserved. Grace is giving blessings and favor when it is not deserved. Joseph showed both grace and mercy to his brothers. He knew that God had been gracious and merciful to him. This is why we too must forgive those who hurt and wrong us- because God has so graciously forgiven us. Jesus said,

Lu 17:3-4 "Take heed to yourselves: If thy brother trespass against thee, rebuke him; and if he repent, forgive him. And if he trespass against thee seven times in a day, and seven times in a day turn again to thee, saying, I repent; thou shalt forgive him."

Joseph is again a picture of the Lord Jesus. Though the Lord Jesus was condemned and mistreated by His own brethren, the Jews, and crucified by the Gentiles; yet, as He hung upon the cross of Calvary and watched as they parted His garments and cast lots for His clothing, He prayed, "Father, forgive them, for they know not what they do." Joseph showed mercy to his brethren though they had done him great wrong. He forgave them from his heart.

In these verses, we see the complete fulfillment of Joseph's first dream. All eleven of his brethren were before him. They "bowed down their heads and made obeisance." Obeisance means to bow and show reverence. This was the exact word Joseph used in Genesis 37 when he told his dream to his brothers:

Ge 37:7 "For, behold, we *were* binding sheaves in the field, and, lo, my sheaf arose, and also stood upright; and, behold, your sheaves stood round about, and made obeisance to my sheaf."

Amazing! God had brought it all to pass just as He had promised. It had surely seemed impossible at the time that Joseph dreamed it. His brothers had scoffed at his words and his dreams. They hated him for them; but Joseph had trusted God to fulfill His word in His time. What a miracle it was when God brought everything to pass! Joseph knew that God had done all of this precisely according to His word.

Joseph cared about his brothers. Though they had done him wrong, he still loved them. He asked about their health and about the health of their father. He knew that God would fulfill every detail of his second dream just as He had the first. He would see his beloved father again. Upon seeing his younger brother Benjamin for the first time in thirteen years, Joseph's heart overflowed. It was more than he could bear:

Ge 43:29-30 "And he lifted up his eyes, and saw his brother Benjamin, his mother's son, and said, *Is* this your younger brother, of whom ye spake unto me? And he said, God be gracious unto thee, my son. And Joseph made haste; for his bowels did yearn upon his brother: and he sought *where* to weep; and he entered into *his* chamber, and wept there."

Joseph loved his brother Benjamin so much. How he yearned to wrap his arms around his little brother and pour out his love upon him. God had been so good and had done so much to fulfill His word to Joseph. Yet, he knew it wasn't yet time to reveal himself to his brothers. That time would come. But first, God would bring Joseph's brothers to the point where they would confess their sin and show true repentance.

Ge 43:31-34 "And he washed his face, and went out, and refrained himself, and said, Set on bread. And they set on for him by himself, and for them by themselves, and for the Egyptians, which did eat with him, by themselves: because the Egyptians might not eat bread with the Hebrews; for that *is* an abomination unto the Egyptians. And they sat before him, the firstborn according to his birthright, and the youngest according to his youth: and the men marvelled one at another. And he took *and sent* messes unto them from before him: but Benjamin's mess was five times so much as any of theirs. And they drank, and were merry with him."

Joseph gave them a wonderful meal. He was seated by himself, and they were seated all together. Joseph had them seated according to their birth order, but showed special favor and love to his younger brother Benjamin. The brothers marveled at how this stranger could possibly know the order of their birth, but they still did not recognize him as the brother they had sold so long ago. Joseph tested them once more:

Ge 44:1-13 "And he commanded the steward of his house, saying, Fill the men's sacks *with* food, as much as they can carry, and put every man's money in his sack's mouth. And put my cup, the silver cup, in the sack's mouth of the youngest, and his corn money. And he did according to the word that Joseph had spoken. As soon as the morning was light, the men were sent away, they and their asses. *And* when they were gone out of the city, *and* not *yet* far off, Joseph said unto his steward, Up, follow after the men; and when thou dost overtake them, say unto them, Wherefore have ye rewarded evil for good? *Is* not this *it* in which my lord drinketh, and whereby indeed he divineth? ye have done evil in so doing. And he overtook them, and he spake unto them these same words. And they said unto him, Wherefore saith my lord these words? God forbid that thy servants should do according to this thing: Behold, the money, which we found in our sacks' mouths, we brought again unto thee out of the land of Canaan: how then should we steal out of thy lord's house silver or gold? With whomsoever of thy servants it be found, both let him die, and we also will be my lord's bondmen.

And he said, Now also *let* it *be* according unto your words: he with whom it is found shall be my servant; and ye shall be blameless. Then they speedily took down every man his sack to the ground, and opened every man his sack. And he searched, *and* began at the eldest, and left at the youngest: and the cup was found in Benjamin's sack. Then they rent their clothes, and laded every man his ass, and returned to the city."

So Joseph allowed his brothers once again to endure a small taste of the suffering he had endured for so many years. They were falsely accused, and then the worst happened- Benjamin was taken for a thief. The ruler's own cup was found in Benjamin's sack. The brothers rent their clothes in grief and were brought back to Joseph's house.

Ge 44:14-17 "And Judah and his brethren came to Joseph's house; for he *was* yet there: and they fell before him on the ground. And Joseph said unto them, What deed *is* this that ye have done? wot ye not that such a man as I can certainly divine? And Judah said, What shall we say unto my lord? what shall we speak? or how shall we clear ourselves? God hath found out the iniquity of thy servants: behold, we *are* my lord's servants, both we, and *he* also with whom the cup is found. And he said, God forbid that I should do so: *but* the man in whose hand the cup is found, he shall be my servant; and as for you, get you up in peace unto your father."

Judah had told his father, that he would be responsible for Benjamin to bring him back to him safely in Genesis 43:9:

Ge 43:9 "I will be surety for him; of my hand shalt thou require him: if I bring him not unto thee, and set him before thee, then let me bear the blame for ever."

So, Judah began to plead with this ruler of Egypt for his brother's life. Never did he dream it was his own brother, Joseph, to whom he cried for mercy. All Judah knew was that their sin had found them out. He said, "God hath found out the iniquity of thy servants..." Judah could not bear to break his father's heart again by failing to bring Benjamin back. He knew the sorrow they had caused their father. This time the grief would kill him. Judah would rather be a bondservant for the rest of his life than to let that happen.

Ge 44:30-34 "Now therefore when I come to thy servant my father, and the lad *be* not with us; seeing that his life is bound up in the lad's life; It shall come to pass, when he seeth that the lad *is* not *with us*, that he will die: and thy servants shall bring down the gray hairs of thy servant our father with sorrow to the grave. For thy servant became surety for the lad unto my father, saying, If I bring him not unto thee, then I shall bear the blame to my father for ever. Now therefore, I pray thee, let thy servant abide instead of the lad a bondman to my lord; and let the lad go up with his brethren. For how shall I go up to my father, and the lad *be* not with me? lest peradventure I see the evil that shall come on my father."

Joseph Reveals Himself to His Brethren:

Judah's pleading to Joseph showed his true repentance. Joseph could hold back no more. It was time to make himself known to his brothers.

Ge 45:1-19 "Then Joseph could not refrain himself before all them that stood by him; and he cried, Cause every man to go out from me. And there stood no man with him, while Joseph made himself known unto his brethren. And he wept aloud: and the Egyptians and the house of Pharaoh heard. And Joseph said unto his brethren, I *am* Joseph; doth my father yet live? And his brethren could not answer him; for they were troubled at his presence. And Joseph said unto his brethren, Come near to me, I pray you. And they came near. And he said, I *am* Joseph your brother, whom ye sold into Egypt. Now therefore be not grieved, nor angry with yourselves, that ye sold me hither: for God did send me before you to preserve life. For these two years *hath* the famine *been* in the land: and yet *there are* five years, in the which *there shall* neither *be* earing nor harvest. And God sent me before you to preserve you a posterity in the earth, and to save your lives by a great deliverance. So now *it was* not you *that* sent me hither, but God: and he hath made me a father to Pharaoh, and lord of all his house, and a ruler throughout all the land of Egypt. Haste ye, and go up to my father, and say unto him, Thus saith thy son Joseph, God hath made me lord of all Egypt: come down unto me, tarry not: And thou shalt dwell in the land of Goshen, and thou shalt be near unto me, thou, and thy children, and thy children's children, and thy flocks, and thy herds, and all that thou hast: And there will I nourish thee; for yet *there are* five years of famine; lest thou, and thy household, and all that thou hast, come to poverty. And, behold, your eyes see, and the eyes of my brother Benjamin, that *it is* my mouth that speaketh unto you. And ye shall tell my father of all my glory in Egypt, and of all that ye have seen; and ye shall haste and bring down my father hither. And he fell upon his brother Benjamin's neck, and wept; and Benjamin wept upon his neck. Moreover he kissed all his brethren, and wept upon them: and after that his brethren talked with him. And the fame thereof was heard in Pharaoh's house, saying, Joseph's brethren are come: and it pleased Pharaoh well, and his servants. And Pharaoh said unto Joseph, Say unto thy brethren, This do ye; lade your beasts, and go, get you unto the land of Canaan; And take your father and your households, and come unto me: and I will give you the good of the land of Egypt, and ye shall eat the fat of the land. Now thou art commanded, this do ye; take you wagons out of the land of Egypt for your little ones, and for your wives, and bring your father, and come."

All the pent up emotions of the years of sorrow and suffering overflowed as Joseph finally revealed himself to his brothers. He wept aloud, and the whole house of Pharaoh could hear as Joseph wept and cried out, "I am Joseph, doth my father yet live?" His brothers were dumbfounded by the shock and fear that overwhelmed them. Joseph was so gracious and forgiving to his brothers. He comforted them and told them to come near to him. God had fulfilled His word. It was God's purpose for Joseph to go ahead of them into Egypt to save them from this awful famine. God meant it for good. The evil they had done to Joseph had been turned for their repentance and salvation. God had used Joseph- the brother they hated -to save them and their families from certain death.

Now, Joseph stood before them with outstretched arms and called them to come near. He offered salvation and abundant blessings to them and to their families. The testimony of what Joseph did for his brethren was told to Pharaoh and to all of his servants. As a result, Pharaoh gave his own provisions to Joseph's family and invited them to come and enjoy the best of the land of Egypt. By God's grace, Joseph provided for the salvation of his family from the grievous famine that ravaged the whole earth. He forgave all that his brothers had done to him, and, instead of revenge, he offered them forgiveness and restoration.

In the same way, the Lord Jesus left His home and Father in Heaven and came into this wicked world to suffer, to die, and to save us from the awful plague of sin. He gave Himself to die at the hands of sinners who hated and rejected Him. Yet, He offers mercy and forgiveness to all who will come to Him in repentance and faith. "While we were yet sinners, Christ died for us" (Ro. 5:8). This is the love and mercy of God. In Joseph's life, God gave us a beautiful picture of His love and forgiveness through His own Son, the Lord Jesus Christ.

Joseph gave his brothers provisions for their journey and wagons to bring their father and families back to Egypt where they would be safe and provided for in the years to come:

Ge 45:25 "And they went up out of Egypt, and came into the land of Canaan unto Jacob their father, And told him, saying, Joseph *is* yet alive, and he *is* governor over all the land of Egypt. And Jacob's heart fainted, for he believed them not. And they told him all the words of Joseph, which he had said unto them: and when he saw the wagons which Joseph had sent to carry him, the spirit of Jacob their father revived: And Israel said, *It is* enough; Joseph my son *is* yet alive: I will go and see him before I die."

The truth of all that had happened to Joseph and all that God had done was finally coming to light. Jacob was overwhelmed. His heart fainted within him. How could it be true? Seeing the provisions sent by Joseph and hearing his words revived Jacob's hope- hope that had been dead for so long. His faith revived, and it is interesting to note, that at the moment Jacob's faith revived, God called him not Jacob, but Israel- the name that God had given him that means "prince with God" (Ge. 32:27-28).

Ge 46:1-7 "And Israel took his journey with all that he had, and came to Beersheba, and offered sacrifices unto the God of his father Isaac. And God spake unto Israel in the visions of the night, and said, Jacob, Jacob. And he said, Here *am* I. And he said, I *am* God, the God of thy father: fear not to go down into Egypt; for I will there make of thee a great nation: I will go down with thee into Egypt; and I will also surely bring thee up *again*: and Joseph shall put his hand upon thine eyes. And Jacob rose up from Beersheba: and the sons of Israel carried Jacob their father, and their little ones, and their wives, in the wagons which Pharaoh had sent to carry him. And they took their cattle, and their goods, which they had gotten in the land of Canaan, and came into Egypt, Jacob, and all his seed with him: His sons, and his sons' sons with him, his daughters, and his sons' daughters, and all his seed brought he with him into Egypt. Joseph's father and all the families of his brethren did come to Egypt."

God had been faithful to Israel. On the journey to Egypt, he stopped in Beersheba, the place where his grandfather Abraham had worshipped so many years before and called upon the name of the LORD, the everlasting God (Ge. 21:33). There Israel worshipped the LORD and offered sacrifices "unto the God of his father Isaac." There God called to Jacob again and confirmed the covenant He had made with his father Isaac and his grandfather Abraham. God would be with him on his journey to Egypt, and one day, God would bring the nation of Israel back to the land of Canaan. Jacob was to go not only to visit Joseph, but to stay there with him for the rest of his life. Joseph's own hand would close Israel's eyes in death.

Jacob's heart had returned to the Lord, and God responded to Israel's heartfelt worship with reassurance of the promise He had given to both His father and grandfather to make of him a great nation. This was also a confirmation of God's word to Abraham that the children of Israel would suffer affliction in a land not their own:

Ge 15:12-14 "And when the sun was going down, a deep sleep fell upon Abram; and, lo, an horror of great darkness fell upon him. And he said unto Abram, Know of a surety that thy seed shall be a stranger in a land *that is* not theirs, and shall serve them; and they shall afflict them four hundred years; And also that nation, whom they shall serve, will I judge: and afterward shall they come out with great substance."

The persecution of Abraham's seed at the hand of the Egyptians actually began with Isaac being afflicted by his older brother Ishmael (Ge. 21:9), but had its complete fulfillment in the bondage of the Israelites in the land of Egypt in the days of Moses. This was all part of God's plan. Joseph was the first to enter Egypt as a slave, but God miraculously delivered him, just as He would miraculously deliver the entire nation of Israel by the hand of Moses many years later.

Israel obeyed the word of the LORD and went to Egypt. Joseph finally saw his father again after all those years. God had fulfilled Joseph's dreams just as He had promised:

Ge 46:29-30 "And Joseph made ready his chariot, and went up to meet Israel his father, to Goshen, and presented himself unto him; and he fell on his neck, and wept on his neck a good while. And Israel said unto Joseph, Now let me die, since I have seen thy face, because thou *art* yet alive."

What a wonderful reunion it was! Joseph had remained faithful and obedient to God even through terrible suffering and injustice. He believed God's promises and kept his heart and his life pure. It was worth it all that day when he saw his dear father again. It is the same in our own lives. We can't always understand why things happen the way they do. Sometimes, like Joseph, we suffer even when we are living to please God. But we can trust the sure promise of God. God will work out His good for us in the end, just as He did for Joseph:

Be An Example

Ps 37:4-5 "Delight thyself also in the LORD; and he shall give thee the desires of thine heart. Commit thy way unto the LORD; trust also in him; and he shall bring *it* to pass."

God gave Joseph the desires of his heart and fulfilled every promise in a wonderful way. In His time, we can trust Him to do the same for us.

"How Firm a Foundation"

How firm a foundation, ye saints of the Lord,
Is laid for your faith in His excellent word!
What more can He say than to you He hath said—
To you who for refuge to Jesus have fled?

Fear not, I am with thee, oh, be not dismayed,
For I am thy God, and will still give thee aid;
I'll strengthen thee, help thee, and cause thee to stand,
Upheld by My righteous, omnipotent hand.

When through the deep waters I call thee to go,
The rivers of sorrow shall not overflow;
For I will be with thee thy trouble to bless,
And sanctify to thee thy deepest distress.

When through fiery trials thy pathway shall lie,
My grace, all-sufficient, shall be thy supply;
The flame shall not hurt thee; I only design
Thy dross to consume and thy gold to refine.

The soul that on Jesus doth lean for repose,
I will not, I will not, desert to his foes;
That soul, though all hell should endeavor to shake,
I'll never, no never, no never forsake.

-Anonymous/Unknown, 1787

Chapter 14: "The Life of Miriam"

Memory Verse:

Php 2:3-4 "*Let* nothing *be done* through strife or vainglory; but in lowliness of mind let each esteem other better than themselves. Look not every man on his own things, but every man also on the things of others."

Scripture Reading: Exodus 1-2

Key Lessons: Courage to act on behalf of others; Faith in the salvation of God

We've studied the life of Joseph- a young man who trusted the Lord through adversity and watched as God fulfilled his dreams in a miraculous way. God used Joseph to save multitudes of people from certain death- including his own family, the children of Israel -during a famine that spread over the entire world. The children of Israel came to live with Joseph in Egypt, where they were nourished and protected by his hand. Years later, after Joseph and all his generation had died and the family of Israel had grown exponentially in Egypt, the situation changed for God's people:

Ex 1:6-22 "And Joseph died, and all his brethren, and all that generation. And the children of Israel were fruitful, and increased abundantly, and multiplied, and waxed exceeding mighty; and the land was filled with them. Now there arose up a new king over Egypt, which knew not Joseph. And he said unto his people, Behold, the people of the children of Israel *are* more and mightier than we: Come on, let us deal wisely with them; lest they multiply, and it come to pass, that, when there falleth out any war, they join also unto our enemies, and fight against us, and *so* get them up out of the land.   Therefore they did set over them taskmasters to afflict them with their burdens. And they built for Pharaoh treasure cities, Pithom and Raamses. But the more they afflicted them, the more they multiplied and grew. And they were grieved because of the children of Israel. And the Egyptians made the children of Israel to serve with rigour: And they made their lives bitter with hard bondage, in morter, and in brick, and in all manner of service in the field: all their service, wherein they made them serve, *was* with rigour. And the king of Egypt spake to the Hebrew midwives, of which the name of the one *was* Shiphrah, and the name of the other Puah: And he said, When ye do the office of a midwife to the Hebrew women, and see *them* upon the stools; if it *be* a son, then ye shall kill him: but if it *be* a daughter, then she shall live. But the midwives feared God, and did not as the king of Egypt commanded them, but saved the men children alive. And the king of Egypt called for the midwives, and said unto them, Why have ye done this thing, and have saved the men children alive? And the midwives said unto Pharaoh, Because the Hebrew women *are* not as the Egyptian women; for they *are* lively, and are delivered ere the midwives come in unto them. Therefore God dealt well with the midwives: and the people multiplied, and waxed very mighty. And it came to pass, because the midwives feared God, that he made them houses. And Pharaoh charged all his people, saying, Every son that is born ye shall cast into the river, and every daughter ye shall save alive."

God had blessed the children of Israel. They had become very prosperous in the land of Egypt. Unfortunately, the Pharaoh at the time of the book of Exodus did not know Joseph. He didn't know about the man that the true God of Heaven had raised up so many years before to save Israel and the entire world, including Egypt, from starvation and destruction. Pharaoh didn't see these "Hebrews" - as a blessing upon his nation. Instead, he saw them as a threat to his power. There is a reason why we need to understand history and reflect upon what God has done. There would have been no nation of Egypt if not for God's salvation through Joseph. But this new king did not heed the lessons of history. He thought he could hold to his power by destroying God's people. God was not going to let that happen. The more Pharaoh and the Egyptians afflicted the Hebrews, "the more they multiplied and grew." Many years before, God had promised Abraham that He would bless the nations and people who showed Abraham and the nation that would descend from him with favor and kindness; but God would curse those who cursed Abraham and his descendants:

Ge 12:1-3 "Now the LORD had said unto Abram, Get thee out of thy country, and from thy kindred, and from thy father's house, unto a land that I will shew thee: And I will make of thee a great nation, and I will bless thee, and make thy name great; and thou shalt be a blessing: And I will bless them that bless thee, and curse him that curseth thee: and in thee shall all families of the earth be blessed."

Eventually, Pharaoh would get a very hard lesson about the truth of God's promises concerning His people. As we've learned before, God always keeps His promises. God made another promise to Abraham about the future of His seed- a promise that was reaching its fulfillment at this very time:

Ge 15:13-14 "And he said unto Abram, Know of a surety that thy seed shall be a stranger in a land *that is* not theirs, and shall serve them; and they shall afflict them four hundred years; And also that nation, whom they shall serve, will I judge: and afterward shall they come out with great substance."

Abraham's seed, the children of Israel, had lived for many years as strangers in the land of Canaan. In the days of Joseph, they moved to Egypt, where they were strangers as well. The affliction of the seed of Abraham by the Egyptians actually began when Ishmael, the son of Hagar, Sarah's Egyptian handmaid, persecuted the promised son of Abraham and Sarah-Isaac. Later, Joseph, Abraham's great grandson, was also afflicted by the Egyptians when he was sold by his brothers to Ishmaelite traders. These traders were descendants of Ishmael. Even then, they were still the persecutors of Abraham's seed. Joseph was sold to the Egyptians to suffer as a slave and prisoner for thirteen years. Though God used Joseph in Egypt to deliver his people from certain disaster, after he died, this king of Egypt who knew not Joseph, enslaved the people of Israel and made their lives bitter with hard bondage.

Pharaoh went even further in the persecution of Abraham's seed. He commanded the Hebrew midwives- women trained to help deliver babies -to kill all boy babies born to the Hebrews. Fortunately, these Hebrew midwives feared God and would not obey this wicked command. We can learn something from the example of these faithful women. We are to obey the human authority over us unless that authority commands us to disobey God. In that case, we are to obey God rather than men. These women showed great courage in what they did. God blessed them for their obedience to Him and gave them families of their own.

God had warned Abraham over four hundred years before that His people would suffer and serve a nation not their own, but God also said that He would deliver His people in a mighty way when the four hundred years were passed. Through all the things that happened to Isaac, and to Joseph, and to the children of Israel in Egypt, God was fulfilling His word perfectly. God would deliver His people out of the land of their persecutors. By the time of Exodus 2, that deliverance was soon coming. The four hundred years of suffering for Abraham's seed were almost over. God would use the faith of one Hebrew family to begin to bring His plan to pass:

Ex 2:1-3 "There went a man of the house of Levi, and took *to wife* a daughter of Levi. And the woman conceived, and bare a son: and when she saw him that he *was a* goodly *child*, she hid him three months. And when she could not longer hide him, she took for him an ark of bulrushes, and daubed it with slime and with pitch, and put the child therein; and she laid *it* in the flags by the river's brink. "

When the faithful midwives refused to kill the boy babies of the Hebrews, Pharaoh commanded his own people to throw the Hebrew boy babies into the Nile River. The whole nation of Egypt became the persecutors and murderers of God's people. Only God knows how many little innocent babies were taken from their Hebrew parents and killed in this manner. But God had a special plan for this little son born to Amram and Jochebed (Ex. 6:20). Jochebed knew that this was a goodly child- a healthy and beautiful little boy. There was something special about him. She determined to hide her little son- and hide him she did -for three months. That in itself was a miracle- that no one revealed that the child was there or perhaps even heard his little baby cries for all that time. The Bible tells us later, in Hebrews 11, that it was faith in God that caused Amram and Jochebed to hide their son in spite of the wicked king's commandment. They would not bend to his evil command; rather, they chose to trust God and hide their child, come what may:

Heb 11:23 "By faith Moses, when he was born, was hid three months of his parents, because they saw *he was* a proper child; and they were not afraid of the king's commandment."

The time came, when the child could no longer be hidden. This faithful Hebrew mother would have to cast her little son into the only place of safety for him- the hands of the LORD. How her heart must have broken as she prepared the little ark of bulrushes to place him in, perhaps never to hold him or to see him again. But there was great faith in what she did.

The ark itself was symbolic- for it was through an ark that God had saved her forefather, Noah, and his family from the worldwide flood that swallowed up everything so many centuries before. God could save her little son too. God gave Jochebed wisdom to make this ark to save her baby. Bulrushes are reeds that grow along the banks of rivers. The ark made of reeds would blend in with plants of the river and provide camouflage for the little boat. God alone would know of the ark's presence in that place until the person of His choosing found Jochebed's son. Bulrushes are a waterproof plant that floats. Boats were commonly made of bulrushes in Egypt (*American Tract Society Dictionary*, "bulrush"). The "slime" held the bulrushes together firmly, similar to mortar between bricks. The ark would not come apart. The "pitch" she covered the inside and the outside with was a resin derived from the sap of trees. It was used on the hulls of ships and boats to make them waterproof (*American Tract Society Dictionary*, "pitch"). No water would leak into this little boat. In every detail, God gave Jochebed wisdom to know exactly how to build an ark of safety in which to hide her little son.

In putting her baby in this ark and into the river, Jochebed was trusting in the salvation of God alone. She put her son into the place that the king had decreed for his death- the Nile River. But to Jochebed, it was the safest place possible, for it was the place of God's choosing. In the same way, God wants us to trust Him with the things and people most precious to us. To the unbelieving Egyptians, what Jochebed did would have seemed to be an utterly preposterous way to save her baby, but Jochebed knew her trust was in the living God. He had saved her people before. He could save her little son as He saw fit.

In the same way, God has shown us His plan of salvation. There is only one way we can be saved. We must trust God's ark of salvation provided for us- the Lord Jesus Christ. He alone can save us from certain eternal death. When we place our trust in Him and in the blood He shed for us on the cross, we have eternal life and a home in Heaven. Jochebed's faith was a wonderful example to us of trusting God's way of salvation.

Be An Example

As we read on in Exodus 2, we learn that another person was present in this situation- Jochebed's daughter, Miriam:

Exodus 2:4-10 "And his sister stood afar off, to wit what would be done to him. And the daughter of Pharaoh came down to wash *herself* at the river; and her maidens walked along by the river's side; and when she saw the ark among the flags, she sent her maid to fetch it. And when she had opened *it*, she saw the child: and, behold, the babe wept. And she had compassion on him, and said, This *is one* of the Hebrews' children. Then said his sister to Pharaoh's daughter, Shall I go and call to thee a nurse of the Hebrew women, that she may nurse the child for thee? And Pharaoh's daughter said to her, Go. And the maid went and called the child's mother. And Pharaoh's daughter said unto her, Take this child away, and nurse it for me, and I will give *thee* thy wages. And the woman took the child, and nursed it. And the child grew, and she brought him unto Pharaoh's daughter, and he became her son. And she called his name Moses: and she said, Because I drew him out of the water."

The little baby hidden by his mother, Jochebed, was Moses, the man who would be used by God to deliver the entire nation of Israel from the bondage of Egypt, just as God had promised. In this passage we learn that Moses' sister, Miriam, watched as he was placed into the river by her mother. Miriam's name is given to us later in the genealogy of Amram and Jochebed's family:

Nu 26:59 "And the name of Amram's wife *was* Jochebed, the daughter of Levi, whom *her mother* bare to Levi in Egypt: and she bare unto Amram Aaron and Moses, and Miriam their sister."

Surely, Miriam had been greatly influenced by her mother's faith. She had probably watched as her mother prepared the little ark of bulrushes and laid her baby brother there. She had watched from a distance as her mother carefully laid the little boat in the river and put her tiny son into the hands of God. Miriam stood "afar off" to see what would become of this child she had come to love and cherish. In her actions, Miriam was a great example of our memory verse-"Look not every man on his own things, but every man also on the things of others" (Php. 2:4). She watched quietly as God's wondrous plan began to unfold. Unbelievably, God would use the daughter of Pharaoh himself- the daughter of the one who had decreed the destruction of her people -to save her brother's life!

Miriam watched as the daughter of Pharaoh and her maids came down to the river's bank. We don't know how much Miriam or her mother knew of this daughter of Pharaoh. But we see here that God touched this pagan woman's heart with compassion for the little Hebrew baby who wept when she saw him in the basket. Of all the people in Egypt who could save this little baby from death, this daughter of Pharaoh could do it. Miriam surely saw the compassion on the face of Pharaoh's daughter and heard it in her voice when she exclaimed, "This is one of the Hebrews' children." Miriam did not hold back in fear, but with great courage, she approached this princess of Egypt and said, "Shall I go and call to thee a nurse of the Hebrew women, that she may nurse the child for thee?" If the princess would take her little brother as her own son, he would be saved from certain death. The princess would also need someone to nurse the baby. Miriam was ready to follow the LORD's guidance just as her mother had. As soon as God began to work, Miriam sprang into action.

The princess not only approved of Miriam's suggestion, she even offered to pay for a Hebrew woman to nurse the child. Miriam went with great joy to bring her own mother to nurse and to care for little Moses. When Miriam brought her own mother back to Pharaoh's daughter, the princess said to her, "Take this child away, and nurse it for me, and I will give *thee* thy wages."

How amazing the salvation of God is! God gave the little son back to Jochebed that she had given up to Him, and He also gave extra provision for her to care for her own son. What joy she must have had to hold her baby in her arms again, and all because she had trusted God. God had used her daughter, Miriam, who cared and acted wisely when God gave the opportunity. Miriam was a faithful daughter who cared for her mother and brother. Because of what Miriam did, her mother was able to nurse her little brother until he was old enough to go to live in the palace as the son of Pharaoh's daughter. Pharaoh's daughter named the child a Hebrew name- Moses -which means "to draw out" or "to rescue" (*Strongs Hebrew Dictionary*).

What a miracle! God used Pharaoh's own daughter to save this child who would one day grow up to be the deliverer of Israel. God would bring His people out of Egypt with a mighty hand just as He promised Abraham. Miriam lived to see this wondrous time of deliverance. Later, in Exodus 15:20-21, Miriam is called a prophetess- one who speaks the Word of God to others. She led the children of Israel in praise to the LORD after their deliverance from Pharaoh and the Egyptians at the Red Sea:

Be An Example

Ex 15:20-21 " And Miriam the prophetess, the sister of Aaron, took a timbrel in her hand; and all the women went out after her with timbrels and with dances. And Miriam answered them, Sing ye to the LORD, for he hath triumphed gloriously; the horse and his rider hath he thrown into the sea."

Personal Reflection:

How Miriam rejoiced to see all that God had done! It all began when, as a young person, she listened to God's voice and cared for others. We can learn from Miriam's example- to look not only to our own concerns, but to be sensitive to the needs of others -in our family, in our church, and wherever God puts us. Then, like Miriam, we can act with courage as God tells us what to do. We have many opportunities to help others or to speak the truth of the Gospel to others. God can give us courage to do what is right if we will open our hearts to His voice and be ready when He calls us to act.

"Ready"

Ready to suffer grief or pain,
Ready to stand the test;
Ready to stay at home and send
Others if He sees best.

Refrain:
Ready to go, ready to stay,
Ready my place to fill;
Ready for service lowly or great,
Ready to do His will.

Ready to go, ready to bear,
Ready to watch and pray;
Ready to stand aside and give
Till He shall clear the way. [Refrain]

Ready to speak, ready to think,
Ready with heart and mind;
Ready to stand where He sees fit,
Ready His will to find. [Refrain]

Ready to speak, ready to warn,
Ready o'er souls to yearn;
Ready in life or ready in death,
Ready for His return.

-A.C. Palmer, 1845-1882

Chapter 15: "The Life of Moses"

Memory Verses:

Heb 11:24-27 "By faith Moses, when he was come to years, refused to be called the son of Pharaoh's daughter; Choosing rather to suffer affliction with the people of God, than to enjoy the pleasures of sin for a season; Esteeming the reproach of Christ greater riches than the treasures in Egypt: for he had respect unto the recompence of the reward. By faith he forsook Egypt, not fearing the wrath of the king: for he endured, as seeing him who is invisible."

Jas 1:2-4 "My brethren, count it all joy when ye fall into divers temptations; Knowing *this*, that the trying of your faith worketh patience. But let patience have *her* perfect work, that ye may be perfect and entire, wanting nothing."

Heb 12:11 "Now no chastening for the present seemeth to be joyous, but grievous: nevertheless afterward it yieldeth the peaceable fruit of righteousness unto them which are exercised thereby."

Scripture Reading: Exodus 2:11-25; 3-4

Key Lessons: Living for eternity; God's preparation time for His servants

God had a wonderful purpose for the little baby boy named Moses who had been saved by his parents' faith and his sister's courageous actions. Moses grew up in the palace of Pharaoh, the King of Egypt, and was raised as a prince by Pharaoh's daughter. What more could a young man want, right? Power, wealth, pleasure- it all belonged to Moses, the offspring of Hebrew slaves. But Moses looked around at all that he had and made a very important and wise choice:

Heb 11:24-27 "By faith Moses, when he was come to years, refused to be called the son of Pharaoh's daughter; Choosing rather to suffer affliction with the people of God, than to enjoy the pleasures of sin for a season; Esteeming the reproach of Christ greater riches than the treasures in Egypt: for he had respect unto the recompence of the reward. By faith he forsook Egypt, not fearing the wrath of the king: for he endured, as seeing him who is invisible."

Salvation and Surrender: the Choice of Moses:

It's hard for us to imagine the situation that Moses found himself in. He lived in the palace of the king. He had every material thing that this world could afford- every luxury and privilege. He was the adopted son of a princess. But Moses knew that his true people were the people of the living God. He looked out beyond this life into eternity and saw a far better purpose for his life than wealth, power, and pleasure for himself. He saw that to live his life for God would bring glory to his Creator and eternal rewards that would never pass away. His choice was clear. He would rather suffer with God's people in bitter bondage and poverty for the rest of his mortal life and spend eternity in Heaven, than to have all the riches of Egypt and spend eternity separated from God in hell. He valued "the reproach of Christ" as far greater riches than all the treasures of Egypt.

We have the same choice to make that Moses made when it comes to how we will live our lives and where we will spend eternity. Have you considered your own life in that light? This life is not the end of things. In fact, it is only the beginning; and none of us knows the length of our days. Our mortal lives are temporary and uncertain; but eternity is forever and sure. There are only two destinations in eternity- Heaven and Hell -and those destinations are determined by what we choose in this life. If we choose to trust Christ as Moses did, we choose Heaven as our eternal home and God's people as our people. Salvation makes an eternal difference. It changes our destination from Hell to Heaven. It also makes a difference in our hearts and how we live in this world. With Christ's presence in our lives, we no longer desire to live for this world, but for God. Have you made the choice that Moses made to trust the Savior and live your life for God instead of for this temporal world and all its pleasures? Would you rather identify with the people of God than to be accepted by worldly friends who don't love and believe in God?

This world and its pleasures will soon pass away. Our life will soon be over. The Bible says in James 4:14, "...what *is* your life? It is even a vapour, that appeareth for a little time, and then vanisheth away." The wealth of this world is like the flowers and grass that soon wither and are gone:

Jas 1:11 "For the sun is no sooner risen with a burning heat, but it withereth the grass, and the flower thereof falleth, and the grace of the fashion of it perisheth: so also shall the rich man fade away in his ways."

The Lord Jesus spoke of the brevity of life and of the folly of living for this temporal world when compared to eternity:

Mt 16:24-27 "Then said Jesus unto his disciples, If any *man* will come after me, let him deny himself, and take up his cross, and follow me. For whosoever will save his life shall lose it: and whosoever will lose his life for my sake shall find it. For what is a man profited, if he shall gain the whole world, and lose his own soul? or what shall a man give in exchange for his soul? For the Son of man shall come in the glory of his Father with his angels; and then he shall reward every man according to his works."

The Lord Jesus saw everything in the light of eternity and so should we. When Christ comes again, He will "reward every man according to his works." The saved will stand before the Lord Jesus at the Judgment Seat of Christ and give an account for how we have lived our lives in this world. This is not a judgment to determine salvation. Our salvation is settled when we trust Christ as Savior. Our sins have already been judged and the eternal penalty for them has been paid. But the saved will answer for the deeds we have done and the life we have lived, whether good or bad. When He returns, we will either be ashamed before our Savior, or we will be rewarded by Him:

2Co 5:10 "For we must all appear before the judgment seat of Christ; that every one may receive the things *done* in *his* body, according to that he hath done, whether *it be* good or bad."

The lost will also stand before Jesus Christ at the Great White Throne Judgment. These who have rejected the work of Christ upon the cross and the salvation He provided will be judged "according to their works." The works that they have trusted to save them will be their condemnation. All of us have sinned and fall woefully short of God's glory. God's standard is not a comparison of one person's work to another's. God's standard is Himself. God is the only One who is good, and holy, and righteous. Goodness is not defined as the best that sinful man can do. That is no goodness at all, for everything we do is tainted by sin. Righteousness and goodness are perfection by their very definition. God alone is good, and God alone is righteous (Mt. 19:17; Ro. 3:12). How does any person compare to holy God? The best works of sinful man are filthy rags in God's sight (Isa. 64:6). That is why no sinner can ever save himself. God alone had to offer Himself as a sacrifice for our sins. At the Great White Throne Judgment, all of the wicked deeds of mankind will be brought out into the open and laid bare before the holy and Almighty God of Heaven, and all of lost humanity throughout history will stand before God. Not one shall escape His judgment:

Re 20:12-15 "And I saw the dead, small and great, stand before God; and the books were opened: and another book was opened, which is *the book* of life: and the dead were judged out of those things which were written in the books, according to their works. And the sea gave up the dead which were in it; and death and hell delivered up the dead which were in them: and they were judged every man according to their works. And death and hell were cast into the lake of fire. This is the second death. And whosoever was not found written in the book of life was cast into the lake of fire."

Re 21:8 "But the fearful, and unbelieving, and the abominable, and murderers, and whoremongers, and sorcerers, and idolaters, and all liars, shall have their part in the lake which burneth with fire and brimstone: which is the second death."

There is not one of us- not one single person -who is not on this list of Revelation 21: 8. We are all guilty sinners before God. You might say, "Well, I'm not so bad. I've never murdered anybody or anything. I don't bow down to idols, and I don't go around lying ..." But what did Jesus say about these things? What is adultery? What is a whoremonger or an abominable person in the sight of God? Jesus said that to look upon a woman to lust after her is to commit adultery with her in your heart (Mt. 5:28). Have you lived your entire life without an impure thought? Have you committed any impure act? Have you ever lusted after something or someone? Have you ever had a thought of murder because you were angry with someone? Murder begins in the heart as well. How many lies do we have to tell to be a liar? What is idolatry? It is worshipping something- anything -instead of the the true God of the Bible and His Son, Jesus Christ. Who are the unbelieving? They are those who have chosen to reject the truth of God. They are those who embrace false religion and trust their own works to save them. They are those who believe the lies of atheism, evolution, rationalism, and humanism. They are those who set themselves up as their own god. They are the hard-hearted members of Bible-believing churches who profess faith in Christ to please men, but in their hearts have no faith in Christ or His Word. Who are the fearful? They are those who fear what others will think of them if they trust Christ as Savior. They are those who fear what they will have to give up to if they become a Christian. Jesus said,

Mt 10:28 "And fear not them which kill the body, but are not able to kill the soul: but rather fear him which is able to destroy both soul and body in hell."

Mr 9:43-48 "And if thy hand offend thee, cut it off: it is better for thee to enter into life maimed, than having two hands to go into hell, into the fire that never shall be quenched: Where their worm dieth not, and the fire is not quenched. And if thy foot offend thee, cut it off: it is better for thee to enter halt into life, than having two feet to be cast into hell, into the fire that never shall be quenched: Where their worm dieth not, and the fire is not quenched. And if thine eye offend thee, pluck it out: it is better for thee to enter into the kingdom of God with one eye, than having two eyes to be cast into hell fire: Where their worm dieth not, and the fire is not quenched."

Christ said it plainly. There is nothing- not even your own body that is worth going to hell for. Eternity is forever. This life is so temporary. Which life are you living for? Have you trusted Christ to save you from the guilt of your sin? Only Christ's precious blood applied to our hearts by faith in His death, burial, and resurrection can take us off the list of Revelation 21:8 and make us pure and forgiven children of God. If you have not trusted Christ as your Savior, you can do it right now. Call upon Him for salvation today while there is still time.

As a Christian, have you determined to serve God with your life rather than to enjoy the pleasures of sin for a season? Are you willing to give up the esteem of the world and suffer reproach with the people of God? Moses looked at that choice. He looked at the lavish palace of Pharaoh- the luxurious surroundings, the abundant food, the beautiful clothes, the satisfaction of every lustful desire -

beautiful women for the taking, pleasure without limit, sports, games, and fun. Then, he looked at his own true people, the Hebrews. They lived in misery, with no freedom. They lived in squalor, and pain, and rigor- in poverty and hard, miserable work day after day. They lived in fear of their lives with no choice and no hope except in Almighty God. Yet, they were the people of the one true God. This God, the only God of Heaven, had promised to deliver them and to send Christ, the Savior and Redeemer, to cleanse them from sin and give them eternal life with Him. Moses looked at that choice and knew what he must do. He would not be called the son of Pharaoh's daughter. He would renounce his worldly inheritance and choose to identify with God and His people. Moses chose wisely. He chose to live his life for eternity. He would give up his status, and riches, and future in this world and instead, bear the reproach of the people who were looking for the promised Christ. Christ's reproach to Moses was better than all the riches this world could give that would soon pass away. Some temporary suffering in this life with eternity in Heaven is far better than the passing pleasures of this life and an eternity in hell. Nothing is worth that.

Moses made the right choice. You may say, "Well, when Moses made that choice, everything went great for him, right? I mean, he did what was right, so the blessings came pouring in, and his life was just perfect since he chose to follow God's way?" Well, not exactly. Moses had to go through a lot of suffering to go God's way. Following Christ means bearing the cross. It means taking Christ's reproach and suffering. But following Christ also gives us a blessing that nothing in this world can ever give- peace with God. Though Moses had to suffer some hard things, God's presence and peace were with him through it all. And Moses' suffering was not without purpose. God used his trials to purify and strengthen him to be the man God could use to deliver His people from the bondage of Egypt.

Purification and Preparation: Moses' in God's School of Training:

The next phase of Moses' life was one of purifying and preparation. It is the same in our lives. If we want to be used of God, we must first surrender as Moses did; then, we must allow God to prepare us for the work He has for us to do. For Moses, that would be a forty year process (Ex. 7:7; Acts 7:23)! Moses made the decision to trust in the God of His people and the promised Christ to come. He turned from the pleasures of sin in repentance and turned to God. At that moment, he received God's salvation. He was counted righteous before God by faith. Then, Moses made the decision to surrender his life to God and identify with God's people rather than the people of this world. Then, God began to work in Moses' life through separation from the impure things of this world. For Moses, the separation was a literal one. He would have to separate from the land of Egypt. That step would come next, and with it, preparation for God's service.

When Moses made his choice to suffer affliction with the people of God, he was eager to do something to save them. He wanted to fix things- to right the wrongs that were causing his people to be in misery. God had to show Moses that he needed some personal fixing before he could help others and become the deliverer that God wanted him to be:

Ex 2:11-15 "And it came to pass in those days, when Moses was grown, that he went out unto his brethren, and looked on their burdens: and he spied an Egyptian smiting an Hebrew, one of his brethren. And he looked this way and that way, and when he saw that *there was* no man, he slew the Egyptian, and hid him in the sand. And when he went out the second day, behold, two men of the Hebrews strove together: and he said to him that did the wrong, Wherefore smitest thou thy fellow? And he said, Who made thee a prince and a judge over us? intendest thou to kill me, as thou killedst the Egyptian? And Moses feared, and said, Surely this thing is known. Now when Pharaoh heard this thing, he sought to slay Moses. But Moses fled from the face of Pharaoh, and dwelt in the land of Midian..."

Ac 7:22-25 "And Moses was learned in all the wisdom of the Egyptians, and was mighty in words and in deeds. And when he was full forty years old, it came into his heart to visit his brethren the children of Israel. And seeing one *of them* suffer wrong, he defended *him*, and avenged him that was oppressed, and smote the Egyptian: For he supposed his brethren would have understood how that God by his hand would deliver them: but they understood not."

Moses was passionate about God's people, but he tried to act on his own. Acts 7:25 tells us that Moses supposed that his brethren would understand that God had raised him up to deliver them by his hand. He knew God wanted him to act on behalf of his people. When he saw an Egyptian striking one of his own brethren, a Hebrew, he defended his Hebrew brother and killed the Egyptian; then he hid the Egyptian's body in the sand. Moses thought he could save God's people single-handed by his own power; but this is not God's way. We can't do God's work without God's power. Moses had holy zeal, but he needed to act with God's guidance and wisdom. God wants us to allow Him to work through us. When we try to do God's work in our own way and in our own strength, the results are always worthless at best, disastrous at worst. In Moses' case, it was disastrous. He had killed a man- granted, it was in defense of a helpless man -but it was not God's way. Word of what Moses had done got around. Later, when Moses tried to intervene and break up a fight between two other Hebrews, they let him know they knew what he had done. Funny thing was, they didn't even appreciate the fact that Moses had intervened to save another Hebrew and killed one of their cruel taskmasters. Instead, they turned on Moses for interfering in their fight! This was just a foretaste of the attitude Moses would have to put up with from some of God's people in future years as their leader. But, at the time, Moses knew one thing- what he had done had been found out. Eventually, Pharaoh himself heard about it and set out to have Moses killed. Moses did the only thing he could do- he ran. He fled from the wrath of Pharaoh into the land of Midian:

Ex 2:15-25 "...But Moses fled from the face of Pharaoh, and dwelt in the land of Midian: and he sat down by a well. Now the priest of Midian had seven daughters: and they came and drew *water*, and filled the troughs to water their father's flock. And the shepherds came and drove them away: but Moses stood up and helped them, and watered their flock. And when they came to Reuel their father, he said, How *is it that* ye are come so soon to day? And they said, An Egyptian delivered us out of the hand of the shepherds, and also drew *water* enough for us, and watered the flock. And he said unto his daughters, And where *is* he? why *is it that* ye have left the man? call him, that he may eat bread. And Moses was content to dwell with the man: and he gave Moses Zipporah his daughter. And she bare *him* a son, and he called his name Gershom: for he said, I have been a stranger in a strange land. And it came to pass in process of time, that the king of Egypt died: and the children of Israel sighed by reason of the bondage, and they cried, and their cry came up unto God by reason of the bondage. And God heard their groaning, and God remembered his covenant with Abraham, with Isaac, and with Jacob. And God looked upon the children of Israel, and God had respect unto *them*."

God had a plan for Moses in that desert of Midian. Moses was "learned in all the wisdom of the Egyptians" and "mighty in word and in deed" as a prince of Egypt, but God would not use him to deliver His people that way. God had to take Moses away from being a prince with worldly power and bring him to a place of being a fugitive and a humble shepherd instead. Moses had to forsake Egypt, not only spiritually, but literally, to become the man God could use. God would deliver His people by His power and would judge the Egyptians just as He had promised Abraham:

Ge 15:13-14 "And he said unto Abram, Know of a surety that thy seed shall be a stranger in a land *that is* not theirs, and shall serve them; and they shall afflict them four hundred years; And also that nation, whom they shall serve, will I judge: and afterward shall they come out with great substance."

God's preparation of Moses took a long time- forty years of leading sheep in the desert was just a foretaste of what Moses would have to do as the leader of God's people. Leading sheep in the desert was the perfect school for Moses to learn to lead the Israelites for forty more years in the wilderness after their deliverance from Egypt. Moses would never have had the patience or learned the dependence upon God he needed if he had not been in God's wilderness school of Midian for forty years. At the time, it may have seemed to Moses as if God had set him aside. He had tried to save God's people, but he had blown it. Could God ever use him again? We don't know how Moses felt about all that had happened to him, but surely it must have seemed to him that his life of service to God was over. His dreams of saving his people must have seemed impossible at that time. Perhaps you've been in a similar place. You want to serve God, but feel you've made too many mistakes for God to use you, or you feel you're in a place of isolation and uselessness. God was not finished with Moses, and if you are surrendered to God and walking with Him, He is not finished with you either. God wants us to yield to His refining process in our lives. For Moses, it took forty years of purifying and preparation (Ex. 7:7). God had an amazing work for Moses to do. He had to make certain that His servant was ready for it. Trials and correction are the instruments God uses to purify His people and prepare them for His work:

Jas 1:2-4 "My brethren, count it all joy when ye fall into divers temptations; Knowing *this*, that the trying of your faith worketh patience. But let patience have *her* perfect work, that ye may be perfect and entire, wanting nothing."

Heb 12:11-13 "Now no chastening for the present seemeth to be joyous, but grievous: nevertheless afterward it yieldeth the peaceable fruit of righteousness unto them which are exercised thereby. Wherefore lift up the hands which hang down, and the feeble knees; And make straight paths for your feet, lest that which is lame be turned out of the way; but let it rather be healed."

God has a reason for our times of loneliness and seeming uselessness. God was preparing Moses for something great out in that lonely desert. And God was hearing the prayers of His suffering people in Egypt. He had not forgotten them. God was bringing His people in Egypt to a place of surrender as well. He would do a wondrous work to bring these two situations together. He would purify Moses to be the most humble and surrendered man- the meekest -upon the earth (Nu. 12:3), and He would answer the prayers of His suffering people in Egypt. God would do this work in a miraculous way and in a very short time. When the time was right, God finally called to Moses, not from a palace in Egypt, but from a burning bush on the backside of the desert:

Ex 3:1-10 "Now Moses kept the flock of Jethro his father in law, the priest of Midian: and he led the flock to the backside of the desert, and came to the mountain of God, *even* to Horeb. And the angel of the LORD appeared unto him in a flame of fire out of the midst of a bush: and he looked, and, behold, the bush burned with fire, and the bush *was* not consumed. And Moses said, I will now turn aside, and see this great sight, why the bush is not burnt. And when the LORD saw that he turned aside to see, God called unto him out of the midst of the bush, and said, Moses, Moses. And he said, Here *am* I. And he said, Draw not nigh hither: put off thy shoes from off thy feet, for the place whereon thou standest *is* holy ground. Moreover he said, I *am* the God of thy father, the God of Abraham, the God of Isaac, and the God of Jacob. And Moses hid his face; for he was afraid to look upon God. And the LORD said, I have surely seen the affliction of my people which *are* in Egypt, and have heard their cry by reason of their taskmasters; for I know their sorrows; And I am come down to deliver them out of the hand of the Egyptians, and to bring them up out of that land unto a good land and a large, unto a land flowing with milk and honey; unto the place of the Canaanites, and the Hittites, and the Amorites, and the Perizzites, and the Hivites, and the Jebusites. Now therefore, behold, the cry of the children of Israel is come unto me: and I have also seen the oppression wherewith the Egyptians oppress them. Come now therefore, and I will send thee unto Pharaoh, that thou mayest bring forth my people the children of Israel out of Egypt."

You'd think after forty years of being isolated in the desert, Moses would have been excited to go do the work God had for him; but he wasn't. Moses had lost his courage. He was afraid. He was no longer mighty in word and in deed with a worldly position of authority in Egypt. He was a fugitive and a humble shepherd. He resisted God's call, and God became angry with him. Yes, he was weak, and that was a good realization. Indeed, he was not up to the task in himself. But God was calling him, and God would be with him. It was now God's power that Moses needed to trust, not his own:

Ex 4:1-20 "And Moses answered and said, But, behold, they will not believe me, nor hearken unto my voice: for they will say, The LORD hath not appeared unto thee. And the LORD said unto him, What *is* that in thine hand? And he said, A rod. And he said, Cast it on the ground. And he cast it on the ground, and it became a serpent; and Moses fled from before it. And the LORD said unto Moses, Put forth thine hand, and take it by the tail. And he put forth his hand, and caught it, and it became a rod in his hand: That they may believe that the LORD God of their fathers, the God of Abraham, the God of Isaac, and the God of Jacob, hath appeared unto thee. And the LORD said furthermore unto him, Put now thine hand into thy bosom. And he put his hand into his bosom: and when he took it out, behold, his hand *was* leprous as snow. And he said, Put thine hand into thy bosom again. And he put his hand into his bosom again; and plucked it out of his bosom, and, behold, it was turned again as his *other* flesh. And it shall come to pass, if they will not believe thee, neither hearken to the voice of the first sign, that they will believe the voice of the latter sign. And it shall come to pass, if they will not believe also these two signs, neither hearken unto thy voice, that thou shalt take of the water of the river, and pour *it* upon the dry *land*: and the water which thou takest out of the river shall become blood upon the dry *land*. And Moses said unto the LORD, O my Lord, I *am* not eloquent, neither heretofore, nor since thou hast spoken unto thy servant: but I *am* slow of speech, and of a slow tongue. And the LORD said unto him, Who hath made man's mouth? or who maketh the dumb, or deaf, or the seeing, or the blind? have not I the LORD? Now therefore go, and I will be with thy mouth, and teach thee what thou shalt say. And he said, O my Lord, send, I pray thee, by the hand *of him whom* thou wilt send. And the anger of the LORD was kindled against Moses, and he said, *Is* not Aaron the Levite thy brother? I know that he can speak well. And also, behold, he cometh forth to meet thee: and when he seeth thee, he will be glad in his heart. And thou shalt speak unto him, and put words in his mouth: and I will be with thy mouth, and with his mouth, and will teach you what ye shall do. And he shall be thy spokesman unto the people: and he shall be, *even* he shall be to thee instead of a mouth, and thou shalt be to him instead of God. And thou shalt take this rod in thine hand, wherewith thou shalt do signs. And Moses went and returned to Jethro his father in law, and said unto him, Let me go, I pray thee, and return unto my brethren which *are* in Egypt, and see whether they be yet alive. And Jethro said to Moses, Go in peace. And the LORD said unto Moses in Midian, Go, return into Egypt: for all the men are dead which sought thy life.

And Moses took his wife and his sons, and set them upon an ass, and he returned to the land of Egypt: and Moses took the rod of God in his hand."

Moses had to surrender his fears and inadequacies to God and obey. God's power would enable him to do the work God called him to do. Perhaps you have fears that hold you back from obeying God's call. Maybe, like Moses, you feel you are slow of speech and slow of tongue. You don't know what to say to people to share the Gospel or you fear to speak publicly for God. That is not an excuse that God will accept. He will give us power, and also will surround us with others who can help us in God's work. God wants our surrender. He made us, and He will empower us in our weakness to do His work. Paul said it this way:

2Co 12:9-10 "And he said unto me, My grace is sufficient for thee: for my strength is made perfect in weakness. Most gladly therefore will I rather glory in my infirmities, that the power of Christ may rest upon me. Therefore I take pleasure in infirmities, in reproaches, in necessities, in persecutions, in distresses for Christ's sake: for when I am weak, then am I strong."

God didn't let Moses off the hook because he was afraid or lacked confidence. He told him to go. He tells us to go as well. He has promised never to leave or to forsake those who trust in Him. When Moses obeyed God and went to his father in law and told him he was returning to Egypt, then God gave Moses the assurance that those who sought his life were dead. Moses had to act in faith in God alone before God told him this. He had to come to the place of Hebrews 11:27, where he would face Pharaoh with God's Word boldly and leave Egypt with God's people, "not fearing the wrath of the king."

Moses, the Deliverer of God's People

Moses, God's man, was finally ready to become the deliverer of God's people. He left Midian and returned to Egypt as God had commanded him, with one serious correction along the way (Ex. 4:24-26). Moses had to obey the LORD in every detail, even in the circumcision of his son. After, this, Moses' brother Aaron, by the word of the LORD, went to meet Moses in the wilderness. There Moses told Aaron what God had instructed him to do (Ex. 4:27-28). Moses and Aaron took God's message to the Hebrew people, and then to Pharaoh himself. God's judgment fell upon the land of Egypt. Pharaoh would not let the children of Israel go free as God had commanded through Moses. Pharaoh hardened his heart against the LORD time and time again, until finally, God hardened Pharaoh's heart to the point of no return (Ex. 9:12; 10:1). It is a fearful thing to continually refuse the LORD.

God sent horrible plagues upon Pharaoh and the land of Egypt, but it wasn't until God struck down all the firstborn of man and beast throughout all the land that Pharaoh finally let the people of Israel leave Egypt. God provided atonement for His own people and protection from death through the Passover lamb on the night that He struck the firstborn of Egypt (Ex. 12). Just as He had promised Abraham many years before, God judged the persecutors of His people and delivered Israel. The Hebrews left Egypt with great wealth. Moses, the humble shepherd of Midian, became the courageous deliverer of his people by the power of God. It all started with Moses' choice to suffer the affliction of the people of God rather than to enjoy the pleasures of sin for a season. Moses went through God's school of surrender and separation, and became a mighty servant of God.

Personal Reflection:

If you belong to God through salvation, He wants to use you to serve Him. Are you willing to surrender yourself to God as a holy sacrifice that He can use? Will you separate yourself from unholy things and allow God to take you through His school of preparation whatever it might be? The Bible tells us that, as Christians, we are to present our very bodies as living sacrifices to God- holy and acceptable to Him. That means we need to clean up before we can really be useful to God. We need to get rid of the things that are impure in our lives and repent of known sin. God's Word explains it this way:

Ro 12:1-2 "I beseech you therefore, brethren, by the mercies of God, that ye present your bodies a living sacrifice, holy, acceptable unto God, *which is* your reasonable service. And be not conformed to this world: but be ye transformed by the renewing of your mind, that ye may prove what *is* that good, and acceptable, and perfect, will of God."

Like Moses, let God have his way with your life. Clean up and surrender to God's preparation process, and see what God will do through you:

"Let Him Have His Way with Thee"

Would you live for Jesus, and be always pure and good?
Would you walk with Him within the narrow road?

Be An Example

Would you have Him bear your burden, carry all your load?
Let Him have His way with thee.

Refrain:
His pow'r can make you what you ought to be;
His blood can cleanse your heart and make you free;
His love can fill your soul, and you will see
'Twas best for Him to have His way with thee.

Would you have Him make you free, and follow at His call?
Would you know the peace that comes by giving all?
Would you have Him save you, so that you need never fall?
Let Him have His way with thee.

Would you in His kingdom find a place of constant rest?
Would you prove Him true in providential test?
Would you in His service labor always at your best?
Let Him have His way with thee.

-Cyrus S. Nusbaum, 1898

Chapter 16: "The Life of Joshua"

Memory Verses:

Jos 24:15 "And if it seem evil unto you to serve the LORD, choose you this day whom ye will serve; whether the gods which your fathers served that *were* on the other side of the flood, or the gods of the Amorites, in whose land ye dwell: but as for me and my house, we will serve the LORD."

Eph 6:12-18 "For we wrestle not against flesh and blood, but against principalities, against powers, against the rulers of the darkness of this world, against spiritual wickedness in high *places*. Wherefore take unto you the whole armour of God, that ye may be able to withstand in the evil day, and having done all, to stand. Stand therefore, having your loins girt about with truth, and having on the breastplate of righteousness; And your feet shod with the preparation of the gospel of peace; Above all, taking the shield of faith, wherewith ye shall be able to quench all the fiery darts of the wicked. And take the helmet of salvation, and the sword of the Spirit, which is the word of God: Praying always with all prayer and supplication in the Spirit..."

Be An Example

Scripture Reading: Exodus 17

Key Lessons: Serving with faith and humility; patience; the armor of God

Moses, the humble servant of God, led the children of Israel out of their bondage in Egypt. God kept His promise to Moses. He brought the Hebrew people out with glorious victory over their enemies. After their deliverance, the children of Israel began travelling through the wilderness toward the land God had promised them- the land of Canaan. Moses was God's chosen leader for Israel, and his right-hand man was a man named Joshua. The Bible calls Joshua Moses' "minister" and "servant." In Exodus 33:11 and Numbers 11:28, we are told that Joshua was young when Israel was delivered out of Egypt. In spite of his youth, Joshua became Moses' most trusted helper. Joshua 24:15 records the testimony of Joshua after years of faithful service under God's leader Moses. God appointed Joshua to be Moses' successor. When God had used Joshua to lead His people into the land of Canaan and had given them victory over their enemies, Joshua commanded them to fear the LORD and to serve Him only:

Jos 24:14-15 Now therefore fear the LORD, and serve him in sincerity and in truth: and put away the gods which your fathers served on the other side of the flood, and in Egypt; and serve ye the LORD. And if it seem evil unto you to serve the LORD, choose you this day whom ye will serve; whether the gods which your fathers served that *were* on the other side of the flood, or the gods of the Amorites, in whose land ye dwell: but as for me and my house, we will serve the LORD."

Joshua led his family and his nation to serve the living God. He set the example for the people and committed himself and his family to serve the LORD alone.

Have you ever had an earnest desire to do something great for God? To be used of God, we must be willing to be diligent in our day to day tasks- in the small, unnoticed things that God has for us to do. God cannot trust us with big things if we are unwilling to be faithful in small things. Every great servant of God in the Bible endured a time of testing or suffering to be prepared to do the great works that God had for them to do later on. They had to be willing to be faithful to God behind the scenes doing the humble work before God used them to do something great for Him. Joshua spent many years as the servant of Moses before he became the leader of the entire nation of Israel.

God had done so many amazing things for Israel. He brought them out of Egypt with a mighty hand and judged Egypt with terrible plagues because they had persecuted His people. He opened the waters of the Red Sea so that the children of Israel crossed through the sea bed on dry ground, then caused the sea to close up, drowning the entire Egyptian army that had pursued them (Ex. 13-14). In the wilderness, God provided His people with water to drink and with bread from Heaven to eat. Sadly, the people of Israel were not very grateful. They did not trust in the LORD even though God had cared for them in so many miraculous ways. They murmured and complained against Moses and against the LORD time and time again. Every time things got hard, they complained. When they got thirsty or hungry, they found fault with Moses and complained against the LORD. In Exodus 17, God again provided the people of Israel with water in the wilderness. God told Moses to strike the rock of Horeb, and when he did, abundant water flowed out of the rock for the people to drink. But the people continued to murmur against the LORD and against Moses. In the midst of all the people's sinful complaining, we read of the faithful young man named Joshua. We never read that Joshua joined with the people in complaining and murmuring against Moses or against the LORD. Instead, he trusted God and helped Moses however he could.

When things get hard, do we complain? Do we try to find someone to blame for our troubles, or do we trust in the LORD and find a way that we can help in the situation? Are we willing to trust God even when the odds seem totally stacked against us? Joshua trusted God to fulfill His word that He would bring His people safely into the land of Canaan. He served God where he was and trusted the LORD to keep His promises.

In Exodus 17, a life and death situation arose for the people of Israel. The Israelites were travelling in the midst of the wilderness on their way to Canaan, when suddenly a well-armed force of people called the Amalekites attacked them. The Amalekites were descendants of Jacob's brother, Esau (Ge. 36:12). They became the bitter enemies of God's people. The Israelites had no physical fortress or shelter in which to hide. They were caught in the wilderness with their wives and children. God alone was their refuge, and the first person that Moses turned to for help in this time of trouble was his young servant, Joshua:

Ex 17:8-13 "Then came Amalek, and fought with Israel in Rephidim. And Moses said unto Joshua, Choose us out men, and go out, fight with Amalek: to morrow I will stand on the top of the hill with the rod of God in mine hand. So Joshua did as Moses had said to him, and fought with Amalek: and Moses, Aaron, and Hur went up to the top of the hill. And it came to pass, when Moses held up his hand, that Israel prevailed: and when he let down his hand, Amalek prevailed. But Moses' hands *were* heavy; and they took a stone, and put *it* under him, and he sat thereon; and Aaron and Hur stayed up his hands, the one on the one side, and the other on the other side; and his hands were steady until the going down of the sun. And Joshua discomfited Amalek and his people with the edge of the sword."

Though the Amalekites were strong and well-armed, Moses knew what the Lord had instructed him to do. God would give His people strength to fight their enemies if they would obey and trust in Him.

The Blessing of Faithful Service:

Moses turned to Joshua and commanded him to choose out men to go and fight against Amalek. Joshua gathered the men and started the attack. While Joshua and the men of Israel were fighting, Moses went up to the top of the hill in Rephidim and raised up his hand to the Lord with the rod of God. As long as Moses' hand was raised up to the Lord, Israel was victorious, but when his hand became weary, and he lowered it down to rest, Amalek prevailed. Aaron, Moses' brother, along with another faithful man named Hur, went up on the hill and put a stone under Moses for him to sit upon; then they each stood beside Moses and held up both of his hands to the LORD until the going down of the sun. Because of this help, Joshua and the men of Israel were able to overthrow and utterly defeat the Amalekites. God gave a great victory to Israel that day because Joshua led the men of Israel to obey and to keep fighting, and Aaron and Hur stood by Moses as he held up his hands to God. They depended upon God's power to help them in the fight. It was not an easy victory. It took a long time, and sometimes it looked as if the battle would be lost, but they did not lose heart and flee from their enemies. They kept fighting until God gave the victory.

The Amazing Power of Prayer:

Through what Moses, Aaron, and Hur did while Joshua and the men of Israel fought the battle, we find an amazing picture of the power of prayer. As Christians, we cannot win any battle without prayer. If Moses had given up and and said, "Oh well, I guess I've prayed enough about that," or "I'm too old and tired to keep going," Joshua and the men of Israel would have been defeated. Joshua fought with all his heart and might, but he couldn't win without the power of God, and this power came only as Moses kept holding up the rod of God, bringing down the power of God to help Israel win. When Moses' arm became tired, he had to lower it to rest. Physical weakness is an ever present reality in this world. Moses did all he could, but he needed help. He needed to rest upon that rock that Aaron and Hur brought for him- a picture of the Lord Jesus Christ. He needed Aaron and Hur, God's other men, to stand alongside him and hold his arms up when they became too weary. This shows us that we need to rest upon Christ and His strength, and we need other Christians to pray with us to continue to hold up our hands to the LORD. It takes prayer, constant prayer, to win the LORD's battles and to strengthen His servants. Faithful, young Joshua and the men of Israel were down there doing the fighting- that was their job. They were in the thick of the battle, but they could not win or have strength to keep fighting without Moses holding up the rod of God. Moses could not have done what he did without those men standing next to him to help. All these faithful servants were necessary- Joshua and the men of Israel to fight, and Moses and his ministers to call down the power of God to help them win.

Thank God for Joshua who led the men of Israel to stay in the battle. Thank God for Moses who held up the rod of God and depended upon His power to gain the victory; and thank God for Aaron and Hur who helped and supported Moses when he was weary. What would have happened if any of these men had not done his part? The battle may have been lost or God would have had to use someone else to do their job. Each person in this situation was important to fulfill God's plan. It is the same today. God has a job for you to do in His service. Are you willing to do it? Or will someone else have to take your place? The job may seem small, but to the LORD it is precious. Each small task for Him makes a difference:

"Little is Much When God is in It"

In the harvest field now ripened
There's a work for all to do;
Hark! the voice of God is calling,
To the harvest calling you.

Refrain:
Little is much when God is in it!
Labor not for wealth or fame;
There's a crown, and you can win it,

Be An Example

If you go in Jesus' name.

In the mad rush of the broad way,
In the hurry and the strife,
Tell of Jesus' love and mercy,
Give to them the Word of Life.

Does the place you're called to labor
Seem so small and little known?
It is great if God is in it,
And He'll not forget His own.

Are you laid aside from service,
Body worn from toil and care?
You can still be in the battle,
In the sacred place of prayer.

When the conflict here is ended
And our race on earth is run,
He will say, if we are faithful,
"Welcome home, My child—well done!"

Refrain:
Little is much when God is in it!
Labor not for wealth or fame;
There's a crown, and you can win it,
If you go in Jesus' name.

-*Kittie L. Suffield, 1924*

No work done for the LORD- in His strength and for His purpose - is insignificant in God's sight. Stay faithful in the place and work God has for you, even if you feel it is small and unnoticed by others. God will make His purpose clear in time.

The Christian's Enemies, Armor, and Spiritual Weapons:

What happened to Israel in the wilderness is a vivid picture of how the devil, the enemy of God's people, attacks and hinders Christians today. Just as the devil tried to hinder the Israelites through temptation, through problems, through complaining, and through the attacks of their enemies, he hinders Christians today. The devil did not want the people of Israel to trust God and go to Canaan where God would bless them and give them the Promised Land. Satan didn't want God's people to rid that land of the wickedness and idolatry the devil had set up there. He threw everything he could at them to get them off the track and destroy them. The devil hates God's people and God's truth. He is always busy, always working against the purpose of God. What if Moses and the few, faithful men like Joshua had decided to follow the way of the devil and the way of most of the children of Israel who griped and complained and didn't believe the Lord? These complainers were playing right into the devil's hands. They wanted to go back to Egypt- back to the world where they had been slaves -rather than go forward with Moses and trust God. And these complainers were the majority. They were following each other and the devil. As we will see, only a very few, including the young man Joshua, followed the LORD completely.

The Bible tells us that the enemies of the Christian are the world, the flesh, and the devil (1 Joh. 2:16; Eph. 6:12-18). We cannot fight these enemies with a physical sword. We must fight them with weapons of the Holy Spirit of God. And we cannot fight them alone. We need God's power and God's people to pray if the battles we face are to be won.

Eph 6:12-18 "For we wrestle not against flesh and blood, but against principalities, against powers, against the rulers of the darkness of this world, against spiritual wickedness in high *places*. Wherefore take unto you the whole armour of God, that ye may be able to withstand in the evil day, and having done all, to stand. Stand therefore, having your loins girt about with truth, and having on the breastplate of righteousness; And your feet shod with the preparation of the gospel of peace; Above all, taking the shield of faith, wherewith ye shall be able to quench all the fiery darts of the wicked. And take the helmet of salvation, and the sword of the Spirit, which is the word of God: Praying always with all prayer and supplication in the Spirit..."

This passage in Ephesians tells us that though there are great spiritual enemies working against God's people constantly, we are not without defense. The Christian has armor and weapons too- both defensive and offensive. We have the armor of God to protect us and to enable us to stand against the wiles of the devil. But the armor is no good to us if we do not put it on. It is a conscious decision to put on the armor of God each day. Satan is very subtle. He has many tricks he uses to try to ensnare God's people. Wiles are tricks and strategies an enemy uses to ensnare a foe. We must be armed and on our guard in order to stand for God. Every part of the Christian's armor is vitally important:

The Belt of truth- This is the truth of God's Word- We must fill our minds and hearts with the truth of the Bible, so that we can be strong in what is right. Our lives must be "girded"- held together -with God's truth. It is the truth of God's Word- trusting it, obeying it –that holds the other pieces of our armor in place. If we are not grounded in God's truth like a firm tree, we will be easy prey to the lies of the devil (Ps. 1; Col. 2:7; Eph. 4:14).

The Breastplate of Righteousness- Pure and right living protect the Christian's heart. Through Christ's power, we are to live according to God's Word. Our hearts are vulnerable to disaster and deception if we are living in secret sin or are compromising with worldly influences. To let sin into our lives is to remove our breastplate. Obedience to Christ is the only way to guard our hearts. If we are living in disobedience to God's Word, our hearts are wide open to the devil's attacks against us. Is there some sin or some influence you are allowing into your life today that you know is not right according to God's Word? Remove it from your life and put the breastplate of right living back in place today. Guard your heart, lest Satan have his way in your life. He wants to wound your heart and hinder your usefulness in Christ's service. Guard your heart with the breastplate of righteous living. Ask Christ to give you power to live rightly for Him today.

The Preparation of the Gospel of Peace- We have a wondrous message to share- the good news that Jesus died and rose again to give us forgiveness and peace with God and an eternal home in Heaven. Are we ready to share it? Do we wake up each day with the knowledge that this is our duty- to share the Gospel of peace with someone who is lost and separated from God? Every soul saved becomes another soldier in God's army and another soul rescued from Satan's power. We are given the charge to preach the Gospel to every creature. This is the battle we are to be engaged in- rescuing souls from Satan's kingdom that they might have peace with God and be part of God's army.

The Shield of Faith- Faith in God is the shield that protects us from the fiery darts of Satan that will cause us to doubt and stray from the Lord. God is faithful. He does not fail. We must trust Him unswervingly and follow where our Great Commander leads. Our peace does not depend upon our emotions or circumstances. It depends upon Christ our Savior. If our faith is in God and His

Word to protect and guide us, Satan's darts of doubt and fear cannot pierce our heart. If our faith is in our own strength, and we stubbornly go our own way, we will surely fall into despair and confusion and be of little use to our Heavenly Sovereign who calls us to the battle. Jesus Christ goes before us. If we keep our eyes upon Him and His power, we cannot fail, though the battle rages all around us.

The Helmet of Salvation- The helmet of salvation is the Christian's identification with Christ. To fail to put on the helmet of salvation is to become careless about the fact that we belong to the Lord Jesus- it is to go AWOL in Christ's service and to live as we please. If we become careless in our living and have no time with our Lord through prayer and the study of His Word, we will forget that we belong to Christ. We have been bought with the precious blood of our Savior. We are His soldiers. He has a claim upon our lives, and we are not our own (1 Co. 6:18-20; 2 Pe. 1:8-9). The Christian who is living for self has forgotten that He belongs to Christ. He has failed to put his helmet of salvation on and is in grave danger of becoming wounded and unfit for Christ's service. The helmet of salvation is the acknowledgment every day that we belong to our Heavenly KIng, and our lives belong to His service.

The helmet is also our assurance of salvation. It is the peace that comes from knowing we belong to Jesus Christ by faith in His shed blood. Salvation is our sure protection against the Devil. We belong to God forever. We cannot be taken out of His loving hand. Nothing can separate us from the love of God that is in Christ Jesus our Lord (Joh. 10:27-29; Ro. 8:34-39). The devil loves to torment God's people with doubt and fear. If we do not keep the helmet of assurance in place, we can be rendered most vulnerable to Satan's attacks. It is a choice to put on the helmet of assurance by trusting in the truth of God's Word. Our salvation does not depend upon our feelings or our own power. It depends upon Christ who can never fail. He has promised that those who come to Him for salvation will never be cast out (Joh. 5:24; 6:37). We cannot be courageous soldiers of the LORD without that helmet of salvation in place. God's Word is our assurance and will protect us from all of the devil's lies.

The Sword of the Spirit and prayer- There are two offensive weapons God's soldiers must use to fight against our enemies- the Word of God and prayer. The Spirit of God does not use clever human philosophy or human wisdom to fight spiritual battles. He doesn't use physical strength. He does not use worldly means and entertainment to change people's hearts. He uses the Word of God:

Ro 10:17 "So then faith *cometh* by hearing, and hearing by the word of God."

1Co 1:18-21 "For the preaching of the cross is to them that perish foolishness; but unto us which are saved it is the power of God. For it is written, I will destroy the wisdom of the wise, and will bring to nothing the understanding of the prudent. Where *is* the wise? where *is* the scribe? where *is* the disputer of this world? hath not God made foolish the wisdom of this world? For after that in the wisdom of God the world by wisdom knew not God, it pleased God by the foolishness of preaching to save them that believe."

2Co 10:4-5 "(For the weapons of our warfare *are* not carnal, but mighty through God to the pulling down of strong holds;) Casting down imaginations, and every high thing that exalteth itself against the knowledge of God, and bringing into captivity every thought to the obedience of Christ;"

Heb 4:12 "For the word of God *is* quick, and powerful, and sharper than any twoedged sword, piercing even to the dividing asunder of soul and spirit, and of the joints and marrow, and *is* a discerner of the thoughts and intents of the heart."

It is the Word of God wielded by the Spirit of God that changes men's hearts. It is the Word of God that gives victory in our spiritual battles. We must become skillful in the use of Word of God to be victorious against the evil forces of this dark world. It was the Word of God the Lord Jesus Christ used against the devil during His time of temptation in the wilderness. It was the Word of God that the apostles used against their persecutors in the book of Acts. It is the Word of God that is our weapon against every enemy- lies, persecution, confusion, doubt, fear, discouragement, and temptation -all these things are cut down by the Word of God through the power of the Spirit of God.

Prayer- This is the other offensive weapon in the arsenal of the Christian soldier. Faithful, persistent prayer is the way to bring God's power to bear in our circumstances in the circumstances of others. It is God's power that can change hearts and events when nothing else can. Faith in God through prayer can move mountains. Prayer can break down impenetrable walls because prayer calls upon God to do what we cannot do. His power can do anything. Nothing is too hard for God.

How God uses His Servants:

Sometimes, like Joshua, we must fight in the thick of the battle against the enemies of the LORD. We are to be the ones out doing the work. Our missionaries are good examples of this. They are in the thick of the battle every day. But we are all to be God's missionaries wherever we are. Like Joshua, we must be willing to be in the heat of the battle doing the Lord's work with all of the strength God gives us. But in other situations, we are like Moses up on the top of that hill. We can't be present in every situation where God is working. We are watching from afar off while the servants of the LORD are doing the work of God in other places. We wish we could be there to help, but we can't be part of the fighting on the ground in every place. In these situations, we are to be like Moses, the man of God up on that hill, lifting up his rod to the LORD. We are to be earnestly praying for God to give the victory to the servants like Joshua who are in the thick of the fighting. We are also to be like Aaron and Hur, who saw Moses' burden and his weariness and the battle being fought down in the valley below. They joined in helping Moses to hold up his hands to the LORD, so that God could give the victory. We are to join with others in prayer and not grow weary until the battle is won. Prayer is as much a part of the victory as the actual working and fighting are, and we are to be just as faithful in it. That's why we are to pray for the servants of God and missionaries in other places. That's why we share prayer requests from other members of our church- so that we can pray for those who are struggling with battles and working for the Lord. When the victory comes, we are part of it too.

Joshua was a faithful warrior, and God gave him and Israel a great victory that day in the battle against Amalek. He was able to lead the army of God's people because he was ready. When trouble came, Joshua was not standing with the complainers. He was standing with Moses, God's man. When Moses told him what to do, he immediately obeyed. Joshua did not stop fighting when the battle got tough. He kept fighting until the battle was won. God was preparing young Joshua for a very important task- to be the next leader for the people of Israel. When God gave the victory over Amalek, He made a promise to Israel concerning this particular enemy of His people:

Ex 17:14-16 "And the LORD said unto Moses, Write this *for* a memorial in a book, and rehearse *it* in the ears of Joshua: for I will utterly put out the remembrance of Amalek from under heaven. And Moses built an altar, and called the name of it

Jehovahnissi: For he said, Because the LORD hath sworn *that* the LORD *will have* war with Amalek from generation to generation."

God promised He would totally destroy Amalek. He told Moses to write this promise in a book as a memorial and to "rehearse it in the ears of Joshua." Moses was to teach Joshua the word of God to prepare him to be Israel's leader. God knew that Joshua would be faithful to lead the people to serve the LORD as Moses had done. Moses built an altar in that place, and called the name of it Jehovahnissi. Jehovahnnissi means "the LORD our banner" or "the LORD our Defender." God would continue to fight against Amalek from generation to generation. He would defend Israel from their enemies, and prepare Joshua to be a leader grounded in God's truth.

Later, when Israel reached the border of the land God had promised them- the land of Canaan -Moses sent twelve men in to spy out the land (Nu 13-14). One of those men was Joshua. Of all the men that went in to spy out the land of Canaan, only Joshua and one other man of faith-Caleb -believed that God would keep His word and bring them into the promised land. These two men trusted that God was still their Defender against their enemies. The other ten men were afraid of the people of Canaan. They convinced the people of Israel that their enemies were too strong for them, and that, in spite of what God had said, they could not go into the land. They were full of fear and unbelief. They even suggested that the people appoint another leader to take them all back to Egypt! The people forgot God's promise that the LORD would be their banner- their Defender. Joshua and Caleb tore their clothes in grief. They couldn't believe that the people would rebel against God after all He had done for them. Joshua and Caleb urged the people to trust God and obey His word:

Nu 14:7-9 "And they spake unto all the company of the children of Israel, saying, The land, which we passed through to search it, *is* an exceeding good land. If the LORD delight in us, then he will bring us into this land, and give it us; a land which floweth with milk and honey. Only rebel not ye against the LORD, neither fear ye the people of the land; for they *are* bread for us: their defence is departed from them, and the LORD *is* with us: fear them not.

Joshua and Caleb told the people the truth of God's Word. They reminded them of the strength and promises of God. But the people only wanted to stone Joshua and Caleb. They were so rebellious against the LORD that God finally told them that all of that generation- from the age of twenty years old and upward -except for Joshua and Caleb -would die in the wilderness. They would not be allowed to enter the land of Canaan. That is exactly what happened. God let them wander in the wilderness for forty years until they all died because of their unbelief and refusal to obey God's Word.

Nu 32:11-12 "Surely none of the men that came up out of Egypt, from twenty years old and upward, shall see the land which I sware unto Abraham, unto Isaac, and unto Jacob; because they have not wholly followed me: Save Caleb the son of Jephunneh the Kenezite, and Joshua the son of Nun: for they have wholly followed the LORD."

God continued to bless Joshua even through that long period of wandering in the wilderness. When the time came for Moses to die, the LORD appointed Joshua to lead the people into the Promised Land. God gave Joshua great victories because he chose to follow the Lord even when he was young- no turning back. As the Bible's testimony says of him, "He wholly followed the Lord." He was a faithful soldier of the LORD who did not quit. If Joshua were with us today, I believe he would have a testimony much like the song, "I Have Decided to Follow Jesus, No Turning Back."

What about you? Will you decide, like Joshua to follow God- no turning back? Will you be a faithful soldier of the cross?

"Am I a Soldier of the Cross"

Am I a soldier of the cross,
A follow'r of the Lamb?
And shall I fear to own His cause,
Or blush to speak His name?

Must I be carried to the skies
On flow'ry beds of ease,
While others fought to win the prize,
And sailed through bloody seas?

Are there no foes for me to face?
Must I not stem the flood?
Is this vile world a friend to grace,
To help me on to God?

Be An Example

Sure I must fight if I would reign;
Increase my courage, Lord;
I'll bear the toil, endure the pain,
Supported by Thy Word.

Thy saints in all this glorious war
Shall conquer, though they die;
They see the triumph from afar,
By faith's discerning eye.

When that illustrious day shall rise,
And all Thy armies shine
In robes of vict'ry through the skies,
The glory shall be Thine.

-Isaac Watts, 1721

181

<u>References</u>

American Tract Society. (1859). *American Tract Society Dictionary: A Dictionary of the Holy Bible.*

Barnes, Albert. (1832-1872). *Albert Barnes' Notes on the Bible Notes on the New Testament, Explanatory and Practical*; Retrieved from *Sword Searcher Software*, version 5.3.

Cloud, David. (2013). *Bible Times and Ancient Kingdoms: Treasures from Archeology.* Way of Life Literature. London, Ont.

Cloud, David. (1993, 1997, 2000, 2002). *Way of Life Encyclopedia of the Bible and Christianity*, 4th Edition. Bethel Baptist Church, London, Ontario.

Encyclopedia Brittanica, "Great Famine, Ireland [1845-1849]." Written by Joel Mokyr. Retrieved from:https://www.britannica.com/event/Great-Famine-Irish-   history.
Orr, James, M.A., D.D. General Editor John L. Nuelsen, D.D., LL.D. Edgar Y. Mullins, D.D., LL.D. Assistant Editors Morris O. Evans, D.D., PhD.Managing Editor, Melvin Grove Kyle, D.D., JJ.D.

Strong, James, S.T.D., LL.D. (1890). *Strong's Greek Dictionary: A Concise Dictionary of the Words in the Greek New Testament; with their Renderings in the Authorized English Version.* Madison, N.J.

Strong, James, S.T.D., LL.D. (1890). *Strong's Hebrew Dictionary: A Concise Dictionary of the Words in theHebrew Bible; with their Renderings in the Authorized English Version.* Madison, N.J.

Webster, Noah. (1828). *Webster's 1828 Dictionary: American Dictionary of the English Language.*Foundation for American Christian Education, San Francisco, CA.

Be An Example

185